Now What?

Navigating Life After Loss

Beth Probst

Published by Book Baby Press.
First Edition

Author's Note

The stories in this book are told as truthfully as I can recall them and based on journal entries I wrote at the time. Occasionally, dialogue consistent with how I remember the interaction has been supplemented. While all persons within this story are actual individuals, some names have been changed and interactions omitted to respect their privacy.

Book cover by Brandi Craig
Book design by Kate Deering

To mom and dad, who taught me the connection between love and loss.

I miss you every day.

Table of Contents

Prologue

The decision was made in an instant but years in the making. "I love you girls but I cannot keep fighting. Please don't be mad."

A glance at the nurse and a final plea from my dad. "Please. I just want to go in peace."

Suddenly we are out of time. After years of ups and downs navigating a broken health care system, watching my dad fight for his life – and win; and advocating for his life more times than I can count, the decision is made. My sister and I advocate for him one last time. We watch dad initiate hospice and support him with all of our heart while our hearts break. He signs the papers instantly. He cannot nor should he suffer for another second in a system where folks fight to keep him alive, regardless of the physical and mental pain he endures and his desire to die. He is ready.

He tells my sister and I he's proud of us one last time in a sterile hospital room. A man of few words, he couldn't have chosen a better ending to a complicated yet rich life. I did not know it at the time, but I will not see him conscious again.

I have anticipated this moment for years. In my head, I had prepared for it over and over again. I made time for visits, listened to my dad's endless stories and jokes, and sought therapy to help navigate the struggles of an aging parent. I worked through my anger surrounding a complicated amputation and a healthcare system that never understood my father.

I resolved all the what ifs in my life – the times growing up where I was too busy pursuing my dreams that I missed the simple things. Weekend fishing trips, county fairs, camping, phone calls and lunches.

I spent the last ten years making up for those moments. I said everything that needed to be said. Yet, I still find myself in this moment, completely lost. Caught in-between. The part where you pray for a quick ending but guilt bubbles up and challenges why you would wish your father dead. A friend who knows grief all too well reminds me there is a difference between honoring your dad's wishes and accepting them.

Later, I am alone in the hospice room watching my dad quickly decline. COVID-19 has added a logistical layer of complications in saying good-bye. Visitors are limited as-is my time. I worry about what the next few days will bring. Science says my dad is on enough morphine that he is comfortable. Logic tells me he made this choice for a reason. He is ready to go. My heart says he knows I am here right now. Here. Sharing one last moment with dad.

I force myself to be present. I tell my dad I love him one last time. That I'm proud of him and he fought a good fight but there was no need to keep fighting. He had made his decision and it was ok for him to let go. As I sit near his bed, I see a man pumped with morphine who has paid his dues and made peace with his decision. There is no fight left, just a desire to join mom in the afterlife. As painful as this moment is, I can almost see him dealing out a hand of cards to my mom with a cribbage board between them. My relationship with faith is complicated, but for now I believe that's where he's headed.

I sit with him until an intense snowstorm makes its way to the area. Visiting hours will end soon and I have an hour to drive. My son needs me home before bedtime. Or, if I'm being honest, I need him. I need to hug him and feel his arms around me before tucking him into bed. It is December 23 and as much as I want to be here, I know there are presents to wrap and food to prep. It is, after all, the most wonderful time of the year, right?

As I get ready to leave the room, I glance at my dad one final time. The nursing staff believes it can be anywhere from hours to a few days. In my heart, I know he will not make it through the night. Decades earlier I sat in a similar situation on Easter Eve with my mom. She too would not make it through the night. The circumstances are drastically different but the scene is eerily similar. My mind fights to not go into overdrive – to start processing all of the logistics that'll inevitably follow. I halt the planner in me and instead say one final goodbye. I pause at the door and look back, ready to say a final I love you. But I stop myself. He knows. He's always known. There is nothing left to say.

I get the call at 3 am on Christmas Eve. He's gone. After 24-years of waiting, he's now joined my mother. The waiting for what's next is over.

Instead, it is replaced with grief. Grief is a crazy beast I'm all too familiar with. A new void in my life no one or thing can ever fill. There will be no story big enough, no fish large enough, or joke bad enough to replace the man who made me.

For a moment, I focus on a higher power and try to believe that dad's struggles are finally over and that he's reunited with mom in time for Christmas. I want to believe Heaven gained another angel this Christmas. Faith is complicated in the face of death. Instead, I only feel a hole in my heart draining whatever energy for life I once had. I don't wake my husband to tell him the news. It would be too real. I call my sister, text my aunt and try to keep breathing. Tears flow freely. I lay in bed anticipating what's next.

Part of me knows what lies ahead. The tsunami of highs and lows that follow losing someone or something you love. The cost of his suffering ending comes with a price that I must pay. I'm an orphan at 42. I immediately dismiss my anger. After all, as Winnie the Pooh once said, *"how lucky I am to have something that makes saying goodbye so hard."*

For over a decade, my dad battled countless illnesses. He came back more times than I can count. My mom's story is similar, I was only 18 when I lost her. In both cases, I knew death was inevitable. Deep down, we all know the finitude of life. It just becomes more real when you experience it.

Experience doesn't make it easier. Despite mourning the loss of my mother for nearly a quarter century, I still struggle with what comes next. How to grieve the right way and meet society's pressure of grieving enough but not too much. How to mourn but move on. As a generation X'er who thrives on facts, I seek the simplest of answers.

When does it get easier?

How long should I be sad for and at what point can I resume life?

Is it ok if I'm still sad anyway?

Why do I hate God right now?

Why did I wish them dead?

Did I cause this?

Why do I resent them for ruining my favorite holidays of the year?

Will I ever stop wondering what is and isn't ok?

How come some people feel their lost ones reaching out to them and I don't?

Should I be questioning my faith right now?

Why do I feel so alone, despite being surrounded by people?

Is this my fault?

Why am I so tired?

Why do I just want things to be normal?

Will anything ever be normal again?

Why is everything so foggy?

Why am I so emotional?

What's the real purpose of a funeral?

Can I just run away?

Why is everyone so annoying?

Why me?

Why now?

Now what?

After months of research and years of living with loss, the questions seem obvious. The answers – unavailable. As time ticks on, I settle into a rhythm of grief suddenly knocking me on my ass, only to a few moments later find myself resuming the mundane crisis in front of me – somehow pushing grief aside. Unexpected laughter and joy would find its way into my life only to leave me feeling ashamed; that some how I haven't paid my sorrow dues in full.

Our brain is miraculous in that one can be at rock bottom in shock and grief while somehow navigating the complexities of parenting in the very same moment. I know experts say you shouldn't multi-task, that it in fact is not a thing, but I believe emotional multi-tasking is the only way to survive.

In some respects, the big losses are predictable. You know they are going to hurt. To love or experience anything meaningful, that's the price of admission. There's also a slew of books by people much smarter than I have attempted to help me navigate these emotions.

There are endless meditations and faith-based support systems that helped walk me through the 5 stages of grief and even told me about a sixth stage focused on meaning in an attempt to help me cope with catastrophic loss. Later, I began to understand that the 5 stages of grief were created for the dying and not the grieving. Catastrophic loss has no rhyme or reason. There is no end point. There is no other side that some books refer to. I know this because I'm living it. Life doesn't get easier, it gets different. You discover a new norm. Life is in fact beautiful and painful. The people and things that cause you the most pain in life, are often those which you loved the most and experienced your most joyful moments.

Here's the thing. I've come to realize that all loss, big and small, hurts. It knocks you off-balance, challenges your identity and at times cripples you into believe you're broken. Other times, it leaves you wondering what kind of human you are for continuing to live, even during the darkest of times. God help you if you compare your loss to the person next to you—their loss is either bigger or smaller depending on the narrative you've created in your head. Your grief is too minimal or too big in comparison to whatever you are grieving for.

Some days, when the loss weighs heavy on my heart, I wish I could wave a magic wand and make it all go away. But what does that even mean? If you erase the loss, does that mean you also erase the person you loved? The problem with anything meaningful is it hurts that much more when you lose it.

Life is a series of gains and losses. A new name, new identity, new friends, new career, often come with a cost. There's that moment of compromise when you settle for what is versus what might be someday. Or, that realization you won't be the next golden girl baton twirler or make the cut for an all-state band. How motherhood challenges your sanity. Or, the stories you tell yourself to avoid working on your shortcomings or celebrating your strengths. The moment you regret letting someone else call your shot. These moments of loss quickly add up, even when replaced with something better.

Sure, you can tell yourself that in order to gain something you must let go. Sometimes you do it willingly. Other times, a force greater than you takes it away. Both scenarios are difficult and remind us that life is hard. It hurts. Even in the most beautiful moments, loss lives in us.

That's what this book is about. A series of stories about loss – ordinary and extraordinary losses – that define us. Starting with the loss of my mother when I was just 18, to a near-adoption, motherhood, marriage, friendships, identity and career struggles—all of these are losses I've carried with me for decades. Loss is inevitable, but that hasn't stopped me from wanting to research and understand the why behind these losses with the goal of healing. I hope to share that wisdom here. Here are some simple, tactical tips and stories on how to lose gracefully; of how to lose, without losing yourself.

I bring no professional credentials or expertise to this book. I am not licensed to do anything other than drive a car. This is not a replacement for therapy. These are simply my stories and some of the lessons I've learned along the way that might help make your road a bit less bumpy. This is not an inspirational story where I reckon with loss, finding God or resolve my feelings of loss. This is a story about being in the trenches and navigating hardship while giving myself grace to find joy as well.

There's an old saying that misery loves company. I hope you find some comfort in these stories and understand that you are not alone in your loss. I believe everyone grieves loss differently but there's value in the collective reality that we all will experience loss throughout our lives. For some odd reason, at least for me, I find peace and comfort in knowing I am not alone when I find I am asking myself over and over again, *now what?*

Chapter 1
The Goldfish

Ten hours after my father died, I found myself in a pet store trying to comprehend the clerk as she explained she could not legally sell my son and I a goldfish due to not having the appropriate tank prepped for the occasion. It was Christmas Eve afternoon and I had promised my 8-year-old son we'd surprise his dad with a fish for Christmas. I was still under the impression that a 25-cent goldfish did not take an act of Congress to secure. In the haste of navigating nursing homes, a global pandemic, a hospital transfer and hospice, I had neglected researching the complexities behind purchasing a simple fish. Standing under the fluorescent lights of the big box pet store, I fought back tears and rage as my mind raced to come up with a back-up plan.

Meanwhile, my son, ever so resilient, immediately suggested we peruse the pet store aisles for a pet we could take home that afternoon. He guided me blindly up and down the aisles, and before we knew it, I was seconds away from making a multi-year commitment to walking out with a hamster. I was all in until my son confirmed that hamster poop was beneath him and that it'd be my responsibility. In that moment, I regained control, fought the holiday crowds and secured four tropical fish, tank, food, and accessories with a few white lies and a lot of grit. We even made it home and had the tank set-up prior to our 3 pm family Christmas zoom call.

The call was unconventional at best. Then again, wasn't that the case with everything during the height of COVID-19? For over an hour, I vaguely stared at my husband's family trying to process what they were saying. I accepted the condolences, while completely numb at the words being spoken. I laughed when others laughed. I did my best to be present but exhaustion was slowly setting in. At some point the call ended. The house got eerily quiet.

I sprang to action, prepping a feast of appetizers my husband and son would soon devour. There is comfort in cooking, a normalcy I needed in a moment where nothing seemed normal. At bedtime, I dig out the gifts Santa had so lovingly stashed in secret hiding spaces and make sure the stockings were stuffed, even for the cat and dog. The pandemic marked the first year we weren't traveling over the holidays resulting in Santa making his way down our chimney on the right day. I collapsed into bed depleted. One day without him now complete. A lifetime to go.

Christmas morning is a blur of flying wrapping paper, toy assembly and giggles. We overindulge in cinnamon bread and bacon. I drink endless cups of coffee, doing my best to stay numb. It doesn't work. My son doesn't understand death the way I do. He willingly accepts grandpa is sick and now dead. Whatever that means. He proceeds to be his usual, bubbly, over-the-top boy. A boy I love so much that my heart busts. As the day progresses, the roller-coaster of highs and lows slowly takes over me. By nightfall, I am exhausted from managing these tidal waves.

A few days later I start to feel the finitude of my father's absence. The clock is ticking. My sister and I need to clean our father's apartment or pay another month of rent. It feels rushed but necessary to keep the process moving forward. It was a lot to unpack or in this case pack up. Residents had questions. Lots of them. They wanted to say goodbye and understand what had happened to their friend and neighbor. We did our best, telling the story as we know it and accepted their condolences with grace, even as we struggled with the same questions. The assisted living manager, who had become his friend, was equally as bewildered.

The reality is, many, many things could have killed my father. He was a recovering alcoholic who smoked for decades and had severe emphysema. He had uncontrolled diabetes and was a recent amputee with another potential amputation on the horizon. He had a collapsed lung, heart and kidney issues, along with an undiagnosed GI bleed that his primary care doctor thought might be cancerous. My dad did not want to know. It was ultimately a hairline fracture in his clavicle that landed him in the Emergency Department two weeks before Christmas. A fracture so small, they didn't even discover it for 2-days. As an amputee, though, that fracture meant rehabilitation in a skilled nursing facility.

A skilled nursing facility that didn't understand the complexities of my father's illness. Rushed admittance with incomplete paperwork that left the facility and the hospital pointing fingers at each other. A global pandemic that meant no visitors were allowed, so families were was unaware of how quickly he was declining. Staff convinced my father's respiratory issues were COVID-19, despite negative tests and x-rays that showed bacterial pneumonia.

One weekend of isolation, high temperatures, low oxygen levels and untreated pneumonia before he was finally admitted to a regional medical center's emergency department unconscious. After a few hours of being on the bipap and a transfer to the intensive care unit before family was finally allowed in to see him and tell him to keep fighting. But it was too late. His will to live? Gone. After 10-years of fighting, this last fight was no longer worth it.

He begged to die versus returning to that facility. He understood that if his shoulder didn't heal, he'd be placed in a nursing home because he'd be unable to transfer himself from wheelchair to bed or commode. A second amputation was imminent with a wound that had festered for nearly a year. There was no end to COVID-19 in sight. It was too much to bear. It all happened so fast and left a lot of unanswered questions.

Cleaning out his apartment, my mind cleared enough to start wondering what happened. A call later with the facility didn't help. My father's primary care doctor reaching out to my sister with questions also made me curious. What happened? Did I do enough? Did we do enough? I thought honoring his final wishes was the right thing to do. Now I feel like a coward. I vow to get answers. I file my questions online with the state's quality improvement department expecting answers within weeks. It would be months before any closure would be provided by those who held the answers to what happened.

Meantime, my sister, and I continue to work through the all-too-familiar to-do list when losing a parent. We meet at the funeral home. Choose the cremation box. Burial won't happen until spring. There will be no funeral. COVID-19 has made sure of that but frankly it is easier this way. My dad always frowned upon funerals – disappointed by those who show up for a free meal when you are dead but aren't kind enough to visit when you are alive. It's a bit harsh but unfortunately true in many instances. My father's assets are distributed. The obituary is written. The condolences acknowledged. New Year's comes and goes. I return to work.

Very quickly, my world collapses. I cannot focus. Life seems extra hard. I find myself feeling lost. I seek out therapy, only to discover that this time, I need to grieve alone. I understand my sadness. I know my therapist cannot make it go away. I just need to live in it for a while. To allow myself time to grieve. To feel these emotions fully, to process them and recognize that my grieving didn't end when the to do list for dad's burial ended. I make a promise to myself to understand what happened but not dwell in his death. Move forward, but ask questions that need to be answered. It is my final promise to dad.

When I make a promise, I keep a promise. Hence the fish on Christmas Eve. I knew with every ounce of my being that I would not return home that day without a fish. I had made a promise to my son and while he would have been fine without a fish, I needed that win. Just like I needed answers to why now. I needed to know that I didn't fall short advocating for my dad after ten years of navigating the healthcare system to ensure he stayed alive. I need to do this while continuing to live my life.

Here's the problem. I keep promises to others. But promises to myself are harder. Have you ever wondered why it is so hard to break a promise to your employer, friend, family, volunteer committee or even random acquaintance on Facebook but promises to yourself are the first to go? If you've figured that out, let me know. I am guilty as charged.

As time goes on, I struggle on a lot of fronts. I find myself with a blank page on what comes next and a lot of questions to answer. Caring for my father at different levels for years consumed a lot of time and energy in my life. Overnight, that space is suddenly empty, a huge void that I have no idea how to fill. It'll take more than a year to answer some of the most basic questions and slowly start filling that page with new hopes and dreams. I've been down this road before. Nearly 25-years have passed since I held my mother's hand as she took her last breath. At just 18, I couldn't possibly comprehend the grief. Now, decades later, I thought I was better prepared. I knew what to expect.

When my mom died, I struggled with my emotions because I was afraid she'd be disappointed in me or people would think I was broken. It was years before I'd really cry or even start to process the impact her death had on me. This time, I realize I need time to ponder. I needed to take time to just sit in the pain.

At one point, I opened my journal and started jotting down simple things I always wanted to try but had been putting off. The list was pretty long. I then pulled up my calendar and with no rhyme or reason, start filling it in. Things I just wanted to do. Not because they'd drive professional or personal growth, or make me look like Mother Theresa or shed 100 pounds. But because it sounded fun. This may seem normal to most folks, but I'm not known for my ability to schedule stuff just for fun, so for me this was a struggle.

Over the course of the year, I'd try rock polishing, enjoy an incredible girl's weekend in the Upper Peninsula of Michigan, plant my first hydrangea, grow massive sunflowers and a vegetable garden of only items I love, take a spin class, resume journaling, devour a stack of smut books, co-coach my son's baseball team and master the perfect margarita recipe complements of Dwayne "the Rock" Johnson and Teremana tequila. I'd train my chickens to come on command with snacks and write out a summer bucket list with my son Jake. It wasn't much, but it was a start to my healing.

It turns this sense of hopelessness and wanderlust has a name. Motivational speaker Mel Robbins calls this productive procrastination. I never knew this existed, only that I was putting off grieving by trying things I loved. Turns out, productive procrastination is allowing one's self space to be creative. It rarely relates to grief, but it is helping me balance the tsunami sized waves of grief that randomly kick me on my ass by giving me the space and permission to be happy.

Sometimes I get to the end of the week exhausted but feeling like I have done nothing. If I allow myself to get caught up in that mentality that to be better than the day before, I need to somehow level up my game, then I am failing on all accounts. Before my dad died, I would have beaten myself up over that, calling myself directionless and without a specific purpose.

Turns out, I was wrong. Sometimes, you just need space to explore. To wander. To give yourself time to figure out what makes you tick. You don't do that by sitting down and envisioning your perfect life and then manifesting it by getting up at 5 am and moving your body. You do it by living. By trying new things and allowing yourself to recognize that you may discover something about yourself you don't know. The truth is, the more I try, the less I know about who I want to be when I grow up but I'm having some serious fun giving myself the space to ask the question. Don't get me wrong, sometimes that even means jumping out of bed at 4:40 am to hit up a local spin class. I did it because I wanted to, not because I thought it'd change my life.

At some point, productive procrastination turns into real action.

Until then, just try something. Catapult yourself into a walk with no purpose other than to check out nature. Wander the aisles of a store and buy something totally frivolous that makes you feel pretty. Buy that extra espresso shot, even if it means you'll end up binge watching an extra couple of hours on Netflix and being tired the next morning. Heck, show up at a spin class and feel like a Rhino riding a bike for the first time, only to leave knowing you've surpassed Lindsey Vonn's trend worthy Instagram #chindrip because you are so out of shape but find yourself wanting to go back for more. You deserve all of that and more, especially in these early moments of loss. I wish I had known this decades earlier when my journey with loss began.

Chapter 2
Intervention

"Moms in rehab. She'll be back in 4-weeks."

I don't recall which family member told me this. I was 15 and had just returned from working at the local video store when I learned an intervention had occurred in my living room earlier that day. Mom was gone. She had been checked in to an in-patient rehab center for alcohol abuse.

I was stunned. At 15, I didn't understand that what was happening in our house was not normal. My mom had been on and off sick for the past four years. She had battled some eating and mental health disorders and I knew she drank a bit too much, but an alcoholic? That didn't seem right.

My teenage brain had compartmentalized her illness as a blip and convinced myself everything was fine. I had bigger problems to handle. I was just a few years away from graduating high school and needed to finalize college plans, secure a second job, enjoy prom and graduate with honors. I was madly in love with a junior who kept breaking my heart by cheating on me with my friend. These were the problems keeping me up at night. Not this.

In three months, I'd hopefully get my license. My plate was full. Mom in rehab? This was not in the plan.

To be blunt, I was tired of this narrative. Of waiting for the day mom might die. A few summers back, my grandma had told me it'd be a miracle if my mom made it to fall without dying. She didn't die. It didn't matter. Pandora's box was open. This idea couldn't be shoved back in the box. I had spent the past few years coming to terms with the fact that any day could be my mom's last day. I avoided fights with her like the plague and always remembered to say I love you when I left the house. I held my breath waiting for the moment she'd be gone.

Somehow, mom dying seemed easier than mom being in rehab. Kids at school are a lot kinder to someone whose mom is dying versus someone whose mom is an alcoholic. For the first time ever, I was embarrassed about my family. I didn't want folks to know. Only my closest friends knew and we normalized it.

A month later, she returned home. She never drank again that I know of but the damage was already done. She'd never fully recover and instead a series of never-ending hospital stays would consume the next few years of my life.

In some cases, in my attempt to normalize this anything but normal situation, I would take advantage of her absences. There was the Friday where I parked illegally in the church parking lot across from the high school. My car was towed. I didn't have the $55 needed to get my car out. My grandma bailed my car out so I could work the night shift at the local video store. Afterwards, I hosted a sleepover at my house. After my dad left to work the overnight shift at the local paper mill, my girlfriends headed to my house. Rather than join them, I met up with my 15-year-old high school sweetheart. I was nearly 17 at the time.

We made out in the sandbox at a nearby playground until his dad's friends happened to ride by on their ATV and busted us. For a moment, I felt like a teenager. Giddy, guilty and carefree. My boyfriend was visibly nervous that his parents would kill him and then me since I was the big city girl corrupting their child. It was a modern-day Romeo and Juliet. Then I noticed the time. I needed to get home or I was in big shit. My mom would soon be calling for her midnight check-in and while my girlfriends would do their best to cover for me, my mom would see right through it. Even in her sickest moments, she somehow knew everything that was going on. Suddenly, the playground debacle seemed like child's play. I mean, what teenage girl wreaks havoc like this when her mom is literally fighting for her life in the hospital? Turns out, this one.

I raced home only to get pulled over for not having the headlights in my 1986 black Ford Escort hatchback turned on. As the cop questioned me for being out so late with no lights on, alligator-sized tears streamed freely down my face, and I found myself warding off a panic attack. He took pity on me and let me go with a warning. It didn't matter. I missed her call.

"I think your mom is on to you," my best friend Cara warned me when I blew into the house at half-past twelve. She did her best to ward my mom off by saying I was in the bathroom. My mom called bullshit. "She said she's going to call back very soon."

Moments later the phone rang. I had nothing to lose. I told my mom the truth about the sandbox escapade. She laughed. Told me she was glad I was safe and that she missed me. We chatted briefly about school. I skimmed over the towed car and warning from the cop, which didn't even seem to register as an issue. Moments later the call ended with her telling me to tell my friends hello and to have them keep looking out for me. My heart broke. Even when I fucked up, it didn't get a reaction.

I had broken curfew, got busted making out in the middle of the night, been pulled over for reckless driving and had a half-dozen girlfriends in our home with nobody watching them but all was well because I was safe. I imagine in the grand scheme of things my transgressions seemed harmless. But they seemed insurmountably dangerous to my rule-following self.

My girlfriends giggled over how cool my mom was. How if they pulled this nonsense in their house, all hell would break loose. Crazy how the grass is always greener on the other side.

I was never grounded. I can count on one hand the number of times I was spanked – the most dramatic being when I attempted to burn down my father's ice fishing house. My parents loved me unconditionally. They believed kids should make mistake—have enough rope to hang themselves while they waited in the wings ready to save us from ourselves if things got too bad.

As a teenager, I was not well-equipped for this freedom. I craved order, boundaries, consequences and accountability. Normalcy. I never got that. Instead, I lived cautiously in the unpredictability of a home with bigger problems than my curfew and boy troubles. It rushed me into adulthood at a time when I wanted to be a kid.

I took this responsibility seriously. I yanked my friend's hair and made her pick-up a can she had littered on a popular walking trail. I accosted my girlfriends who dared to drink Zimas underage. I never cheated on a test and questioned the integrity of my classmates who attempted to program the elements chart in their TI-85 calculator versus doing the work to memorize the table or accept the consequences of not acing chemistry. I read every page of Les Misérables even though the cliff notes version was readily available. I even completed the optional homework just in case.

After my mom returned home, she encouraged me to take an afternoon off of school. I was working two jobs and after school activities had left me burning the candle on both ends. I was fearful of getting caught. She convinced me otherwise. I escaped for an afternoon of rollerblading on a nearby bike trail. Unbeknownst to me, my mother had called the school to pull me out. The simple miscommunication highlighted that I was skipping school. I spent the following week eating lunch in the cafeteria, my freedom of open lunch stripped from me by an unrelenting principal who was all too familiar with my rule-breaking sisters. I would try skipping school one other time to road trip up the north shore of Minnesota with one of my best friends only to get caught by my band teacher. He saw us pumping gas at the station versus being in English. While he didn't report us, he had a chat with us about what kind of example we were setting as leaders of the program. I was devastated.

This is what happens when you break the rules. Your freedom goes away. For years, I played the role of rule follower. I determined that if I followed the rules, everything would work out. I believed I had that power. I began tiptoeing through life aiming for perfection knowing that at any moment life could fall apart. Sure, mom was now sober. But she was still sick. I was smart enough to know that one more drink could be her last. A simple program didn't make her disease go away.

Sober mom fought hard to stay alive, but she was riddled with health issues. I became accustomed to the rotary phone hanging in each classroom my junior and senior year ringing. Each time, I knew it was quite likely a call letting me know mom was back in the hospital. I became numb to it. I accepted this was my life.

I did everything I could to keep life together. I rarely argued with my mom, swallowing any teenage angst and anger, fearful that we'd fight, and she'd die. Despite knowing she was proud of me, my fear of failing became all-consuming. I fought hard to be smart enough, pretty enough, good enough, only to find myself falling short. Falling short against my own judgement and allowing other people's opinion define me. This would only intensify after she was gone.

Our last lucid conversation was a screaming match about laundry. It'd be decades before I'd find the courage to forgive myself for being human.

Looking back, I wish I could have granted my teenage-self permission to break the rules. To laugh more and cry less. To embrace the joys of being a kid. To recognize that skimming a chapter, skipping a class or walking away from the high school clubs you hate don't make you a failure. It makes you human. That boys will break your heart if you let them, but that your worth should not be wrapped up in their opinion of you. Acne is a rite of passage. It means you are morphing into an incredible woman that'll go on to do great things. You will never need to know the elements chart. Someday if you choose, you can read the unabridged version of Les Mis or attend the musical. Nobody will judge you for that, or if they are, they should not be a part of your life. Life is hard enough without making it more difficult by adding perfectionism to your to-do list.

Chapter 3
The Funeral

There are few things I remember about my mom's actual funeral. Sitting front and center, I played the role of devastated daughter. Tears openly streamed down my face as I held back silent sobs. In that moment, I wasn't mourning the loss of my mother. My 18-year-old brain simply couldn't process she was gone forever.

Instead, my inner critic was replaying in my head over and over again the last interaction I had with my mom. It involved folding laundry. I was a typical teenager who didn't want to listen to her parents. The only problem is my mom had been pretty sick for several years so it was hard to pull the selfish righteous indignation play on someone who is actively dying. I had years of pent-up rage inside of me that fateful Good Friday.

My mom had just come home from yet another surgery. She wasn't feeling well, even though days before I had heard the surgeon say the surgery went well. I was tired and looking ahead to the dayshift at the local video store followed by a night shift at Hardees. The last thing I wanted to do was haul laundry upstairs and help my mom fold it. I let her know it.

What I didn't realize was that not feeling well meant she had an infection. What I didn't realize as I shouted, "fold your own laundry" and fled the house is that it'd be the last thing I'd say to her consciously. I didn't know that twelve hours later my uncle would walk into Hardees and tell me my mom was back in the hospital and they didn't think she'd make it.

I'll never forget that moment. To this day, it still seems surreal. I didn't believe him. My mom was invincible. She survived an eating disorder, defeated her inner alcoholic demons, and battled mental illness all while raising three daughters and maintaining her marriage. I was wrong yet again. She'd die on Easter Eve after a last-minute attempt to remove the infected shunt from the surgery that was going to make her better. The surgeon couldn't save her but she didn't die. Left on life support, our family had no choice but to make the tough call.

That final day is hazy at best. I know I spent a few moments with her alone, in which I did my best to tell her everything that mattered. I recall a tear falling on her face and in my memory, her opening her eyes and telling me not to cry. That she wasn't dead yet and she'd always be with me. Memories are funny that way. Logic says that didn't happen. It couldn't have happened. Yet, I carry that memory with me everywhere I go.

Just before midnight, our family would gather round her one last time and watch the heart monitor, awaiting that final beep. Looking at her one last time, she seemed peaceful. Ready to let go. I was not. I'd spend years grappling with how and why this happened to me.

Funeral planning occurred in a haze of compromise, attempting to meet the conflicting demands of those who loved and knew her best. I quietly listened in as we planned the final act of my mom's life, telling myself I had lost my right to plan anything when I spewed enough hate to kill her. I know now that's insane, but at the time, it was easier to hate myself for her dying than grieve her loss.

I wasn't a regular at funerals but was familiar enough to dread the inevitable. You know, the people that'd tilt their heads and say they were sorry before sharing stories over dry sandwiches and scalding hot coffee. The people that'd scrutinize my every move, worried that at any point I might breakdown, all because they loved and cared for me. The semi-strangers who would offer an awkward hug as a consolation prize for me losing the person that birthed me. Wistful prayers and uplifting church music. The overwhelming scent of endless flowers. It was too much.

The morning of the funeral, I remember practicing my funeral face. I didn't want to seem too sad or melancholy, but also feared being judged for smiling that this dreadful day was almost over. I wanted to get this one right. If not for me, for my mom. She deserved this. She deserved a daughter who would honor this final act of her life. Yet, to do so, I needed her here with me. I fretted over what to wear, yet struggled to get dressed. A part of me wanted to run away to my favorite State Park and honor her the way that made sense to me. Instead, I armored up and headed to the Lutheran Church I grew up in.

Walking into the sanctuary and seeing my mom's casket surrounded by a field of flowers, every emotion I've been holding in starts to boil beneath the surface, ready to blow. The stoic Scandinavian in me pushes them down so deep that barely a tear comes out.

My grandma glances at me nervously and puts her arm on my shoulder, "it is ok. Just let it all out."

My head is racing. I know there is a part in the script I've missed. My acting job has failed. This is where the youngest daughter is supposed to break out in tears and mourn the loss of her mother. Instead, I feel nothing. It'd be weeks before the walls would see their first crack and I would experience my first mournful panic attack. It'd be years before I'd finally seek therapy and allowed myself to mourn her loss. For now, I wasn't ready to process it. It was too much, too soon. Even now, decades later, I'm still surprised by what moments trigger an overwhelming response of grief – both positive and negative. The brain is funny that way.

I think to the five stages of loss. It is the only education I have on this unsettling feeling. A narrative that often plays out seamlessly in movies. Denial, anger, bargaining, depression, acceptance – if only I can make my way through these stages, I'll be able to move on. Given my unwillingness to feel anything, I surrender to being in denial. What I didn't understand then is that Elisabeth Kübler-Ross built her five stages of grief for those who are dying, not those left behind. These stages, while universal emotions one might expect to feel when losing something or someone they love, do not happen in order and despite what Hollywood would tell you, they do not end. There is no other side to grief. There is just a time when you eventually can function again, in spite of your grief. It'd take me decades to truly understand this.

On this day, I choose to believe I'm in denial and that this too shall pass. That at some point, life will return to normal. As the funeral progressed, I avoid grief by relying on rage. Tears streamed down my face, but they are ones of anger not loss. I'm angry at the world and in this moment, God, but I need something more concrete to take my rage out on. I need someone to blame and that someone is me.

I turned inward and cursed myself to hell over and over again for our fight, while my aunt bellowed out the lyrics to *On Eagle's Wings*. It is a beautiful song and she is an incredible singer, but to this day, that song brings me nothing but sadness and despair. A reminder of some of my darkest moments.

I quietly sat in the guilt of believing I was the reason she was gone until the bible verses, religious hymns, sermon and prayers come to a close. The service ends and we slowly leave the sanctuary amid a sea of eyes watching us. I cannot get away from her and this place fast enough. I am granted a mini-reprieve before the second act of funeral day starts.

I take a moment to hide, wondering how long I can postpone human contact. Alone in my thoughts, I find the grief too hard to process. I return, only to find myself passing by the sanctuary. There, in the back pews, my friends are quietly chatting. I don't know who or what they are talking about, but I find myself jealous that I'm an outsider. Prom is just around the corner and high school graduation is just two months away. College decisions were being announced and high school romances were coming to an end nearly daily. It could have been any one of those things. All I knew was I longed to be in their circle talking about someone or something else.

I casually strolled up hoping to crack one of my dry, sarcastic remarks about whatever flavor of the day they were chatting about, when suddenly their voices dropped. Smiling faces turned neutral. Heads tilted. The intention was to remind me that they were here to support me and to love me. That while they had all experienced loss of their own at some level, they didn't want to pretend to know what I was going through or present a solution. Instead, I felt like the alien green monster who smelled funny and couldn't find her place in the world.

Awkward exchanges played out. Nobody knew what to say. The more I asked about real life, the more uncomfortable the exchange became. Everyone was there to help, only I didn't know what help I needed. I honestly couldn't even tell you if I had showered that day. The only thing I knew was I wanted to be them and that was not an option. My role on this day was as an outsider.

I am eternally grateful for the amazing friends in my life. They did and continue to stand by my side as I flounder along trying to figure out which end is up. I just wished in that moment I was not the motherless daughter but instead the high school senior planning which dorm she'd be staying in come fall. In that moment, I wanted to be an 18-year-old girl stressed about whether the guy she liked would ask her to prom and be busy coordinating my graduation party versus my mother's burial. This was not an option. Days earlier Jesus had risen from the grave as my mom made her way to her final resting place. Now, I was stuck in the aftermath trying to make sense of my faith, friendships and future.

My mother's funeral was full of well-intentioned people full of sympathy. I felt their pity and their sadness and their desire to make my pain go away. What I needed more than anything in that moment was empathy. I just wanted someone to really understand how lost I was feeling in that moment. I craved connection more than anything but few could relate to the overwhelming sense of loss and emptiness

I was experiencing.

Dr. Brene Brown talks a lot about difference between sympathy and empathy, stating that in times of loss, "the truth is, rarely can a response make something better. What makes something better is connection." As someone who lived it, I couldn't agree more. Connection is hard – especially when one of the individuals is struggling to function. But, anything is better than the pity party that often occurs at a funeral.

To this day, I struggle with funerals. It seems an awful burden to put on people in shock and so often the focus is sympathizing with those left behind. It is tending and caring for how others feel versus taking care of your needs. Worse yet – a celebration of life. As if in just a few days of someone leaving you forever, you can party like it is 1999 and celebrate their life versus taking a moment to acknowledge a life without them in it. Talk about pressure. As if there isn't enough guilt processing all of the tumultuous unanswered questions that come with losing someone you love.

My mom's funeral was no exception. It was an incredibly lonely day. Despite being surrounded by family and friends, I felt misunderstood. I longed for solitude only to fear my thoughts if left alone. I longed for the day to be over so my life could return to normal. I pushed too quickly return to high school, resume my jobs, and immerse myself in the final extra-curriculars with high school graduation. It'd be years before I began to truly understand the impact of losing such a pivotal person in your life.

The funeral marked a pivotal before and after moment for me. The before Beth believed in herself. A bit cocky perhaps, but believed in her heart that she could in fact set out and do anything she wanted.

She was ruthless, loud and full of life. The after Beth, not so much. The after Beth carried a lot of anger. Anger assured there wasn't space for heartbreak. Anger fueled my desire to prove myself to anyone and everyone who would listen. That somehow, if I did that, I could make up for what I did. That if I was just a little more perfect, a little less human, then I'd never hurt someone the way I hurt my mom. This would lead to a series of relationship mistakes, empty promotions and endless schooling, as I kept reaching for more and believing it'd never be enough.

Until it was. At some point, grief has a way of catching up with you. Nearly a decade later, I'd finally step into a counselor's office and share my deepest secrets. I'd slowly start to piece my life back together. I often wonder how different life would be if I hadn't waited so long. If I had not only acknowledged my grief sooner but sought help with someone to process it.

I can play a serious game of what ifs. It is a dangerous game full of outcomes that cannot be proven or disproven. Maybe I would have forgiven myself sooner and perhaps some of life's bigger hiccups wouldn't have hurt quite so much. At what cost, though?

The truth is, the greater the connection, the harder the loss. My mother gave birth to me but she also loved me unconditionally. I wouldn't truly understand what that meant until I became a mother myself. Our relationship was complicated, weighted down by the reality that she would in fact die at just 47. That experience changed me. Hardened me, perhaps.

It is hard to balance the complexities of teenage angst and high school heartbreak with the harsh reality of a less than perfect mother navigating demons and the illness they brought. My high school journals reflect on lunchtime fights and acne issues to mom's medications and rehab, often times in the same paragraph. Unbeknownst to me, the brain has a phenomenal way of normalizing whatever we are exposed to. In hindsight, I can now respect and understand the walls I built to keep moving forward, despite the chaos around me.

I'm no longer angry at myself. Sad at times for what I didn't know or understand. For missed opportunities and milestone moments I am forced to experience without my mom. I'm also grateful. It is that same experience that brings me here to share these words. It was her death that allowed me to pursue my dream of college and a job in my field and to never settle. It was those choices that would later lead me to moving to Wisconsin and falling in love and becoming a mother and building a beautiful life for myself and my family. It was her death that made me realize at an early age, life is in fact finite. There isn't always tomorrow. The present moment matters.

These lessons would play out over and over again. I realize now that grief and joy go hand-in-hand. To truly love, you must also lose. It hurts, but much can be built from pain. It would take 25-years of me aiming for perfection and failing regularly to understand that nothing I did or accomplished in life would erase that fateful fight. That no matter how much I wanted to believe I was living out my life in honor of my mom, what was truly happening was I was punishing myself over and over again for something completely out of my control. My mom was an alcoholic. Somehow, I found the strength and courage to understand her illness and forgive her long before I forgave myself. Forgiveness is an incredible tool that we often find space to give others but rarely ourselves.

Chapter 4
The Waterfall

Two months after my mom died, I found myself standing on a bridge, staring into a rapid, root beer colored river contemplating what's next. This bridge, located on a former railroad turned bike trail, was a spot my friends and I often went to do the things innocent teenagers do.

There was the time my friend dropped her pants for my French foreign exchange student after asking him if he wanted to see a full moon. Or, the time that a Park Ranger busted my boyfriend and I making out after hours in the nearby State Park. We skipped rocks, shared stories of love and heartbreak and talked about our future. We ate candy, slammed Dr. Peppers, and carefully treaded into the rapids for a quick swim. We had picnics, late night walks and maybe even a skinny dip or two in this river.

Today, I am alone. In a few hours I'll receive my high school diploma in front of family and friends. Then, I'm off for a two-week cross-country adventure with my favorite friends performing a contemporary Christian musical and living out of an oversized van. When

I return, I'll work full-time at the town's paper mill trying to save up money to supplement the student loans I'll need to pay for college. Then, I'm off pursue life on my own terms. These adventures, while daunting, scream freedom and fun. In this moment, I feel nothing but shame.

Grief is odd that way. At times, tsunami sized emotions hit me. I never know when to expect them, or how to handle them. They are unpredictable. Sometimes I catch myself laughing at a joke a friend made and hate myself for not holding on tighter to my grief. Or, I feel my mom's presence and wait for the tears to flow only to find myself grateful that she's moved on. That the timing of her death opens the road for me to travel this summer and attend college next fall, not fearing I'll be absent at her death. Other days, there's nothing but pain—where even the simplest of tasks feels like pouring salt on an open wound. I find myself in these moments, filled with rage, cursing her for leaving me with so many unanswered questions. I hate her for making me angry and am fearful that she'll be disappointed that I'm sad or allowing such ugly feelings over and over in my head. The truth is, living with her illness was complicated. But this new normal is simply impossible.

Addicts are often taught the acronym HALT. It stands for hungry, angry, lonely and tired. These four cornerstones are critical to one's overall health and wellbeing, and so addicts are often told they should not make critical decisions or HALT when feeling these because they can result in relapse.

The same rings true in grief. Grief is an incredible stressor in life. Many things trigger it. We are taught to plow ahead. Toxic positivity puts a timeline on our grief. I wish that weren't the case. Great grief is a result of great love. Despite the loss, there is no timeline, just an ability to function. Understanding triggers and taking basic care of one's self is foundational to ever feeling normal again. I wish I had understood this while standing at the waterfall. It'd be over 25-years later when I learned this acronym while watching a Sex and the City remake. Instead, I did everything in my power to table these mixed emotions. It was my attempt to put this pain on layaway until I was emotionally strong enough to process it.

Solitude seems to be the only way to survive right now. I find comfort by water—perhaps that is the Pisces in me. I stare at the turbulent waters below me and try to play out how the next 24-hours will go. A part of me feels my life is on display. My friends and family have already hinted to me how hard this day will be without mom. As if I need a reminder of who I'm missing. They are ready to support me, love me, comfort me in what is sure to be a difficult day.

I feel an inherent pressure to get today right. To grieve her loss at the appropriate level. Yet, in so many ways I welcome today's distraction. I am excited to receive my diploma and stay up all night eating my weight in sugar and celebrating the last 18-years of my life. I worked hard to wear the honor roll ribbons on my purple gown. I don't want today to be about her. The past 4-years have been about nothing but her and her needs. I'd like today to be about me.

This desire scares me. I find myself wondering if this selfish desire somehow breaks the rules of grief that have been engrained in my brain. That somehow, if I celebrate today, I will somehow have moved on. I will have moved past loving the women that made me. The woman that remains an integral part of my life. The woman I do not want to live without.

I look to the river for answers. It bares none. Instead, the rapids drown out my grief. The continuous flowing of water reminds me that time does not stop for grief. The clock keeps ticking. I find myself wondering how it'll feel when two months becomes two years and two years becomes two decades. Will I still remember the sound of her voice? The advice she so wisely shared with me at the most opportune moments? The love she had for her family? How she canned pickles and made a mad flat jack?

I fear forgetting but dread remembering. The wound is too fresh to revisit now. Now, I need to figure out how to get through today. How to embrace what I've worked so hard for while not ignoring the empty seat that'll be at graduation.

A few hours later I'll return home where my father is anxiously pacing the kitchen. He casually asks about my where-abouts, an unusual question in our household. I look to his face and see a sea of worry. I don't ask him what he's thinking. I can feel his pain.

"Is everything ok," he asks?

It is a simple question. One that months earlier resulted in me oversharing stories about my boyfriend who cheated on me… a third time. His response at the time,

"I thought you were the smart one. Why do you keep going back to him?"

I was so angry at dad in that moment. How dare he give me advice about the boy I love. Granted, it was solid advice and the guy didn't deserve another second of my heart. What I'd give for that to be the context of this question today.

Instead, my father and I bond over our unspoken grief. Will we ever be ok, I think to myself?

"I'm good," I respond.

In that moment, I can almost convince myself I mean it. For just today, I try to forget my new found reality and just be a teenager.

My dad seems relieved by my response. The neighbor stops by to help me iron my graduation gown. It is one of many life lessons I never had a chance to learn from mom. My grandparents and sisters arrive. We snap some photos. We make small talk. I head to the high school.

There, nothing about the evening is about my mom. It is about the life my fellow graduates and I have spent the past 18-years living. We laugh and cry and share memories. We throw our caps, a final moment of high school rebellion. Afterwards, we enjoy an all-night party that symbolizes the kick-off into adulthood but is spent reliving much of our youth. Many happy tears are shed.

Driving home the next morning, I'm elated yet exhausted. It was in fact the perfect day. Walking into the house, I stop by my mom's room without thinking. Perhaps it is the fact that I've been up for 36-hours or the power of habit, but I throw open the door ready to say, "mom, you won't believe what happened last night."

In an instant, I'm reminded. My mom's belongings remain untouched. It'd be months before we'd clean her room out. Unopened books I had given her for Christmas sit next to her bed. Family photos and a framed version of Elizabeth Barret Browning's Sonnet 43 adorn the bookshelf above her now empty bed, *"I shall love thee better after death."*

A crack in the numbness knocks me off my feet. I slink to the floor and bury my head in my hands. I realize she's never coming back but I will continue living. A gap begins building between the moments we had together and the ones I endure on my own.

I find myself telling mom anyway about the guy Mike I just

met and how he'll soon be deployed to Bosnia but there's something about him I like. How he's mysterious and kind and boldly serving his country. I also know due to his deployment; we'll never get close and therefore he cannot break my heart. I laugh about the liters of Dr. Pepper I slammed and the funny old-time photos my friends and I took at the all night graduation party. I tell her how excited I am for my two-week upcoming adventure where I'll travel cross country with friends in a 15-passenger van performing a Christian musical while living on church floors. How I'm nervous about paying for college and more importantly fitting in and finding my voice. The conversation flows freely, after all, what can mom say in return? No longer sick, I can finally speak to her unfiltered about my life, my dreams, my hopes and fears.

In movies, this is often where a ghost appears and reassures me everything is going to be ok. Or, I have some spiritual awakening and closure. My reality is different. She doesn't appear or tell me everything is going to be ok. I realize that part is now on me. But somehow, talking to her in this moment makes it less real. It allows me to believe that maybe she can hear me. Maybe she can help me. Maybe there's a meaning to this madness that I do not understand. For now, that is enough.

It is in this moment that I start to understand that you don't stop loving someone when you lose them. My 18-year-old-self thought that to get through my grief, I needed to let go of my mother. To get to the other side. But honestly, what does that even mean? I don't want to let go of the 18-years we had any more than I want to live the rest of my life without her. Yes, she's physically gone. My relationship with faith is complicated. Yet, my love for my mom remains and nothing about that ever has to change. Likewise, I never have to stop missing my mom. My grief doesn't have a timeframe. The reality is, I can keep living my life and still mourn my mom. The two aren't mutually exclusive. I can even experience joy again while still wishing my mom was here on Earth to bear witness to it. This lesson will play out over and over again throughout my life.

Chapter 5
The Coin Toss

Waterloo, Iowa. I was 21-years old and had successfully navigated college. I'd be graduating in a few months with a degree focused on broadcast journalism and I had somehow managed to manifest an interview in a mid-size television market in the land of cornfields. The stakes were high. Despite having an extremely exciting and productive internship near home, there were no producer jobs available. This first-generation college student had a lot to prove. I needed to land a job in my field.

The alternative – the local paper mill where my father worked his entire career and I spent my college summers working was hiring. I was practically guaranteed a slot. After spending four summers pushing buttons, cleaning machines, and other miscellaneous jobs I knew I was not cut-out for mill work. I didn't have the heart to tell dad and instead prayed for a miracle.

I started sending out countless unanswered resumes in the fall. I bolstered my resume and called my shot. I wanted to be in television news management. I wasn't an on-air wannabe but a serious journalist who loved working behind the scenes and after interning for two summers and working at the local PBS station in college, I was ready to shine.

Turns out, in 1999, there were thousands of eager graduates just like me who had attended accredited colleges and understood that cover letters carry you only so far. They had polished resume tapes and professors with connections. I attended a 4-year college with an unaccredited journalism program and had next to no career advice. The cards were once again stacked against me.

An overpacked schedule and taking college courses in high school meant I was graduating in December. I was running out of time and job seeking during the holidays. A bad combination. I needed a new strategy. I pulled out a map and looked at the markets closest to Duluth that had job openings. Fargo, North Dakota and Waterloo, Iowa. I called the news directors at both and asked if I could spend time with them. I shared my passion to learn more about their station and what they looked for in a producer. I thought if I just got my foot in the door, they'd want me to join their team.

Derek from Waterloo took pity on me. He didn't offer to pay my expenses or even ask for a resume. Instead, he made time on his calendar to meet with me. I didn't care. My naïve 21-year-old self believed he'd hire me. After all, there was a morning produce slot open that was perfect for me. I roped my girlfriend into the idea that a road trip to Iowa could be our Thelma and Louise moment. She immediately went all-in. The stars aligned.

Driving into Waterloo, I asked if I could make this place my home. It was the week before Thanksgiving break and the stark, snow-covered corn husks in the open plains of Iowa screamed adventure. My father had also suggested that if I moved to Iowa, I might marry a farmer and if I did, he best hunt pheasants. I won't lie. The idea of an Iowan farm boy seemed mysterious and romantic all at once. Plus, what Midwestern girl doesn't dream of owning her own John Deere?

After checking into our hotel. I drag my friend to the mall searching for the perfect power outfit. I didn't own a traditional suit and jacket and knew I had one shot to make a first impression. I drop $150 in a big box store that I don't have on a serious looking charcoal gray suit and blue button-down shirt. At the cosmetic counter, the Clinique gal persuades me to purchase an overpriced foundation that I also can't afford. I keep telling myself, you have to spend money to make money.

The next morning, I watch the morning news and take notes on what I'd do differently. I throw on my new power suit and recognized it was Go Time. Only I don't want to go. I am scared shitless of failing.

"You're going to knock it out of the park," my best friend Cara exclaims. "You always do. I don't even know why you are worried."

This, coming from the girl that defines fearless. I wish I could channel her confidence. Instead, I take her well wishes and channel my best what would Cara do energy for the meeting.

I immediately take a liking to Derek, the news director who took pity on me. We sit down in his cluttered office packed with resume tapes. I ask him some questions about what he looks for in a producer. He seems mildly amused and shares what he's looking for in the new staff he hires. He starts talking about the morning show.

This is my moment. I start making some comments about the show from the notes I had made that morning. Some were over-the-top compliments and some were suggestions on how I might improve graphics to strengthen teasers. I do my best to sound confident but not arrogant. The reality is, I really had no clue what I was talking about but it worked. Something piques his interest to keep chatting with me well past our designated time.

He asks me if I had my resume. While I'm not a boy scout, I'm prepared. I pull out my resume and the entire script of a newscast I produced in the last week of my internship. I explain to him that the news director at Duluth trusted me to write and booth the summer show.

Derek seems skeptical. "You produced this show or wrote a script for it," he asks.

"I wrote it."

This is a bit unconventional for an intern in the 90s but the station was small and after 3-months of begging, I was allowed to produce a 10 pm newscast, partially because nobody else was available due to a heavy vacation schedule. I left the part out about everyone being on vacation and just explained that I had earned the trust of the team and they wanted me to walk out of the internship with a tape in hand.

The dynamics of the conversation shift. It became more about my experience, my desire to produce and what I could bring to Waterloo. Questions about whether I'd actually relocate and thoughts about my long-term plans were exchanged. Derek talks about Waterloo being a feeder market for larger stations and stations that could help me achieve my long-term goal of being a big city news director. Suddenly, our time is over.

As we part ways, Derek apologizes for not having planned this out better. He should have made time for me to meet other team members and sit in the booth during a newscast. I tell him I cannot stay. The reality is I cannot afford another night in Waterloo. As fun as this adventure is, I'm broke and this conversation has set me back several hundred dollars. As I go to exit, he asks if it is ok for him to check my references. It is then I realize, this might become my new home.

"How'd it go," Cara asks. She knows she has a 7-hour drive with me and a crabby Beth is never a good Beth.

"Good, I think." I then go into overdrive, replaying the entire conversation. "Cara, my first job, could land me in a top 100 market. Who needs Duluth when I can be in Waterloo?!?!"

By the time I arrive home, there's a message from Derek to call me. I do. He offers me a two-year contract producing the morning news. I'd start as soon as I graduated. I'm ecstatic. He tells me to take the weekend to think about it and let me know.

I go out that evening to celebrate. I'm moving to Waterloo, Iowa! I return home after dinner and my dad says, "your new boss called and ask that you call him tonight."

"Derek?" I ask. It is after 8 pm and that seems odd.

"No, John. He said he'd be at the station until at least 10 pm," my dad explains.

I'm super confused. John was my old boss. I know he's at the station because of the annual parade they produce which means all hands on deck. But John assured me just a few weeks ago that there were no jobs open for me. He anticipated a producer leaving within 3-6 months but until that happened, he couldn't even consider hiring me.

I dial the newsroom without thinking twice.

"Are you ready to come work for me," John asks.

"Huh?"

"Derek called me. I gave you a good review. But, when I told the producer team, they said I better offer you a job. I'm pretty sure one is leaving really soon. We want you on our team. You can do the morning show and even the noon show," he explains.

In my head I'm thinking, the morning show doesn't have a producer. It is virtually a rerun on the previous night's news managed by the anchor and weather guy. The noon show is similar. The salary offer is even worse.

"We can offer $16,000 to start," he says. Derek's offer is $26,000.

"Is there any wiggle room on that?" I ask.

"I can look into that. Take the weekend to think about it and let me know Monday. We'd love for you to start the week of December 20."

That's finals week, I think to myself. I wonder if I'll even have any. My schooling really consists of a thesis presentation at this point so I figure I can make that work.

I tell John thanks and hang up the phone.

I'm at a crossroads. Twenty-four hours ago, I was contemplating whether I'd end up working at the local paper mill and live at home for the rest of my life. Now, I can work at a station I know and love or go create new dreams in some Iowa cornfields. I'm immediately overwhelmed.

I explain the situation to dad. He asks about salary. He logically points out that the Mill's starting wage is more than double what John is offering plus a Cadillac healthcare and a 401k plan. Not to mention the safety that comes with being a union member.

He means well. He's putting my safety and well-being ahead of everyone else. That's all he's done his entire life. It isn't that he doesn't want me to pursue my dreams. He just doesn't understand why I wouldn't find those dreams working the same job he did his entire life.

I realize I need to make a list. To remove emotion and use logic to make the single biggest decision of my adult life. The pros and cons cancel each other out. I go to sleep no closer to a solution.

I spend the next two days avoiding the decision. I drink a bit too much at the bar and pick up a couple extra shifts at Hardees. Anything to not think about where I should go while at the same time hoping a sign will tell me what to do.

Monday morning rolls around. I'm smart enough to know that inaction could result in me losing both job offers. There's a line of talented producers standing in my shadow who would happily take the offers in a heartbeat. They are more qualified than I am. More polished. More prepared. The clock is ticking.

I make a silent plea to mom for help. She doesn't answer. It isn't that she doesn't sometimes speak to me from her grave but instead, her silence reminds me that this is my decision to make. My gut and my brain tell me to follow my heart.

"What does that even mean," I exclaim to an empty room. "Fuck it, it is decision time."

I grab a coin, pick up the phone and call Waterloo. As the phone rings, I flip the coin. Heads, I'm taking the job in Waterloo. Tails, I'm taking the job in Duluth. I'm uncoordinated. In my attempt to hold the received and catch the coin it bounces out of my hand and rolls under the recliner.

I'm shoving my arm under the recliner to slide the coin out when Derek picks up the phone.

"Good morning, Beth! So are you coming to Waterloo," he says, more in a statement than a question.

I glance down at the coin. Tales. Shit. What if this is the wrong decision? My mind races. Is there a stall tactic I can come up with? Should I ask more questions? What do I do? Turns out my mind and my mouth are working against each other.

"I've decided to turn down the job Derek."

He's clearly confused.

"Is it money? I can probably get you some more if that's the case," he says.

"No," I pause. I think to myself, what should I tell him? And the only thing that comes to mind is the truth.

"I've actually decided to work at the station in Duluth. I'm so sorry I wasted your time," I explain.

Derek is likely annoyed but gracious in his response. After all, I had begged him to let me drive to Waterloo to meet him, only to now say I'm not interested in a really great job offer.

Derek quickly accepts my decision. He wishes me the best. A few years later I'd reach out to him when I was ready to move on to a larger market. I'm not sure if he remembers me or I'm just lost in a pile of resumes. He never returns my calls.

I call John. He knows I'm going to say yes before I even say it. I try to play it cool.

"After much thought, I've decided to continue building my future with you."

"I knew you would," he says.

I'd spend the next 5-years of my life pouring my heart and soul into television news. I rarely second guessed my decision and while the hours and pay were mediocre, the experiences and friendships I made were priceless. The news director believed in me. I was safe.

But sometimes, especially towards the end, I found myself wondering what if?

I built a beautiful life out of this choice. This decision also had me belicving I was never quite good enough. On paper, nobody saw my value. I didn't get hired until someone else believed in me. I didn't advocate for more money or recognize my value and was just grateful for whatever was given. I still struggle with this. I'm intensely loyal to an employer – a trait that is detrimental to negotiating raises. I understand that everyone is replaceable and never want my ego to leave me unemployable. Perhaps that is why I have never not had a job since the day I turned 15. It is also the reason I've never gambled big on the decisions that matter.

I find myself wondering what if I had dared to dream bigger when I was mobile. The only thing holding me back was my fear of failure. That if I had gone to Waterloo, would I have been more ambitious and motivated and committed to fulfilling my dream of management. Would I have demanded what I was worth?

I made a choice. For much of my 20s, I lived in limbo land. Not good enough to call my shot but paralyzed about changing course due to fear of failure. I had a plan and pivoting wasn't an option. I did the best I could but I'd be lying if I didn't say I had regrets.

For nearly a decade, I played it safe. I partied a lot, serial dated unavailable guys and took some unnecessary risks that are my secrets to keep. I balanced this out with getting a master's degree, promoted at work and winning some journalism awards. Somehow, I thought the two would cancel each other out. That if my professional life was moving forward, then I could ignore the personal mess I was living in.

The truth is I was stuck. As much as I wanted to believe that this career was right for me – that all the hard work and energy I had invested in the past 10-years was not for nothing – I knew in my heart this was not my life's calling. When it came time to move on to a larger market, I doubled down in Duluth by buying my first home. At some point, my boss questioned what I was doing. It was a piss or get off the pot moment. It wasn't that he wanted me to go. I think he knew I couldn't continue to stay. I was blessed in this moment to have a great mentor that was willing to give me a little push when I needed it most. To acknowledge that the life I had built, despite how hard I had worked for it, loved it and wanted it, wasn't the life for me.

Once I acknowledged this truth, that perhaps I had made a misstep in my career planning, doors opened up for me. I realized that I no longer had to live off the 10-year plan I made when my mom died and instead live life in the moment for me.

This time I wasn't afraid. Always the planner, I had secured a master's degree during my party years. I use my lunch break to apply for a position at an environmental liberal arts college in northern Wisconsin. It is 90-minutes from my hometown (and dad) but allowed me to stay on the shores of Lake Superior.

The human resources department at the college calls within 24-hours. I have an interview the following week. I buy another power suit and polish my writing samples. I drive into Wisconsin recognizing this is a chance to start over. To get serious. I interview well. I immediately connect with the college president. An offer is presented the next day.

This time I don't hesitate. There is no coin flip. No second guessing. I'm scared to start over but it is time to take a chance and bet on myself. It is time to figure out who I am and what I want.

The truth is every gain comes with a loss. In order to start a new life, you must be willing to give up parts of your old life. Seems silly now but in my 20s, I thought I could reinvent myself while not letting go of the current version of myself. It took me nearly a decade to determine my inaction was in fact a choice that was holding me back from creating the life I craved.

Chapter 6
The Cell Phone

It is time. Walking up to the brightly lit kiosk counter in the Miller Hill Mall in Duluth, I bravely stated the words "I need to upgrade my individual cell phone to a family plan."

Granted, I didn't have a family. I had a serious boyfriend that I met after moving to Wisconsin. Serious enough that we shared the same mailing address. Given our frugal nature, we did the math. This plan could save us some serious change. Serious being about $15 per month but when you're living by the words of Warren Buffet, every penny counts.

The sales rep looks at me, looks at my finger, looks at the dude standing next to me and said, "Are you two married?"

"No."

He sighs and pulls out a stack of papers larger than my double spaced, wide margin senior thesis.

"I need to tell you if you do this and break-up, you would still be contractually obligated to pay for his phone plans or break the terms of this contract."

"That's not an issue," I confidently replied. "We're not planning to break-up anytime soon."

I realize now how naïve that sounded. Whatever. Love does that and this was the next natural step in our budding relationship.

"Nobody ever thinks they are going to break-up. You need to know, though, that this contract is binding regardless of whether you two are still together."

What an ass, I think to myself. Do we look like the type of couple that isn't going to make it? I reassure him again that we've talked this through and that I want to add a line to my plan. That this was in fact my choice.

He shakes his head and begins filling out the paperwork. It is painstakingly slow. The endless questions start. Date of birth, social security number, driver's license, credit scores, security questions, passwords, mailing addresses, pins. My head is spinning. We're still on page 1. He runs our credit score. The interrogation continues.

Twenty hours later, aka 15-minutes later, we're approaching the end of the paperwork. I'm sweating. I don't have a fitness tracker on but I'm pretty sure my heart is going to explode. My mind is in overdrive and everything is closing in around me. Things are getting real.

I'm losing my identity. I'm no longer an individual but part of a family. A commitment so real that it apparently takes a courtroom to break it. I start to second guess my decision. As we come to the end of the contract, I find myself stalling. I excuse myself to find the nearest restroom where I hide in a bathroom stall taking a much-needed break.

If I love him, why does this seem so difficult? It is just ink on paper, right? It isn't like I'm turning my life over to this guy. I'm just signing a 3-year contract. A contract that for a few hundred dollars (that I don't have), could theoretically be broken. But I'm a person that keeps my promises. This promise, in-particular, seems very real. It isn't just gaining a family contract but instead losing a sense of myself.

Seems dramatic? Perhaps. So was this contract though.

I ponder this notion for a minute and it starts to make sense. My entire life, my identity has been wrapped up in being someone's other. Sister, daughter, friend, girlfriend. Always someone's other. It wasn't until I moved away for college and enjoyed portions of it single that I started to understand my identity. I suddenly became simply Beth. I was no longer tied to someone or something else. I was just me.

Who is that? A first-generation college student who cut ties and decided to pursue my own dreams. Even when my mom died, I decided to dream big and go to college anyway, even though it would have been easier to stay stuck in my past. Over the course of my 20s, I made many questionable choices trying to figure this whole me thing out. I think I had ten quarter-life crises by the time I was 25. The key being I. I made these choices on my own—sometimes quite selfishly.

I was sitting in a bathroom stall about to give it all up to be someone else. I realized I wasn't concerned about breaking the contract. I knew the guy standing out there was the one. I knew we would survive the toughest of challenges, even a multi-year phone contract, if given the chance. I was concerned about losing myself in the process.

Over the years, this has happened time and time again. I find myself struggling with the balance of being part of something greater than myself while still honoring myself. As a stoic Scandinavian who thrives as an introvert, my individualism matters to me.

I was once told you cannot have your cake and eat it too. For a while I believed that. I now know that's simply not true. Instead, you just have to open yourself up to the fact that there's more than one cake in life. You can in fact buy two cakes and eat one and save the other. You can in fact be a part of an incredible relationship and still stand alone as an individual. Not everything is an either-or option. That said, life is a series of choices. You get to define what matters, but then you must work for it. Marketing guru and all-around brilliant human being, Simon Sinek has a quote I wish I knew back during this conversation. In his book *Start with Why*, he says, "no one likes to lose and most healthy people live their life to win. The only variation is the score we use. The metric is relative but the desire is the same."

In other words, you decide what winning looks like. Not somebody else. If you want to be the girl that falls in love but keeps her independence, you can do that. You just have to find the right guy. Unfortunately, it'd take years and another round of therapy for me to realize that. In the meantime, I take one baby step forward to committing to the man I love.

I head back to the kiosk where my boyfriend and cell phone sales rep are waiting. I boldly sign the contract and never look back. That was over 15-years ago. I still have that cell phone number. We outlived the contract, the college rep's first sales job, and the kiosk now abandoned in the mall. We've since changed carriers and are no longer locked into an unbreakable multi-year cell phone contract. The family plan remains. Savings now in the thousands, tucked away for a rainy day.

As for me, I occasionally still struggle with my identity. Perhaps most daunting was what I lovingly referred to as my thriving thirties. What a shitstorm of highs and lows, all in a decade. Ones you think you can anticipate, and in many cases long for, but society does a great job of masquerading into something else.

There is of course the biggie—my status. I went from girlfriend to fiancé to wife and mother. Each time, I discovered my beliefs and understanding of what unconditional and unwavering love means were completely underrated. You hear about the sacrifice that comes with parenting, often when you are rolling your eyes at your parents, but experiencing it is a whole different ballgame. Talk about high highs and low lows. There really needs to be more about the tough days, because frankly I've never experienced something more challenging than raising a family.

My career took a backseat—something I never thought would happen. I changed jobs three times in my 30s, only to discover that while I know I want to make my mark in the world, I have no clue how to do it. Career advancement, which seemed to come so easily in my 20s, came to a screeching halt as I realized that living in a place I love, doesn't always come with abundant economic opportunities.

The lifelong learner in me had a near meltdown when I finally paid off my student loans and realized for the first time in 34 years I wasn't attending or paying for continuing education. I opted to re-enroll for my fourth college degree, creating a seamless transition from being a student to graduating at the same time my son entered school.

Then there was the pursuit of happiness. Despite self-help books telling me that I could in fact wake up every day and conquer the world and be happy, I seriously question the sanity of those so-called authors. Living the life that I want with those I want, where I want, means compromise. It means prioritizing and sacrificing and wiping boogers and changing diapers. It means long commutes, limited shopping, befriending Amazon Prime and fighting over things like uncrushed diet Mountain Dew cans scattered around the house. It means experiencing unmet dreams and acknowledging that sometimes life is bigger than your needs and wants.

Nobody warned me about the weight-gain that comes with an aging metabolism. Gone are the days of downing Dr. Pepper and munching on chips and Top the Tater while binge watching the latest season of Dawson's Creek. Instead, I found myself hitting the pavement and crossing the finish line of dozens of races yet barely maintaining the weight gain that I'm lovingly calling my dirty thirty in honor of my attempts to do Beach Body on demand at this size. Running highs and lows are a whole different book, but if you had told me in my 20s, I'd have some of my heaviest and hardest conversations with myself wearing running shoes, I would have laughed.

My 30s did not result in endless afternoons hanging out at coffee shops chatting about the weather like the characters on Friends. Instead, it was spent scrambling to keep connections with lifelong friends on Facebook messenger and recognizing that many of those friendships would fade away, despite noble and in some cases knockdown, drag down attempts to keep them. It was hard to let go at times but I find friendships now are easier—more based on common interests, shared values and day-to-day life experiences than the baggage of what I was once pegged to be.

Somewhere in all of this, I discovered that one of life's greatest gifts arrived for me in my 30s. It frankly couldn't have happened sooner. Maybe I'll change my mind after my next existential crisis, but in this moment, I'm still a bit in awe. When I moved to the

Northwoods of Wisconsin, I was ready for change. It was time to abandon my bad habits, face my demons and acknowledge that the person I was trying to be in Duluth wasn't in alignment with who I wanted to become. By the time my 30s hit, I discovered that instead of trying to be someone or something, I could instead be me.

Better yet, I could embrace it. There's something empowering about grabbing life and saying, I'm good enough. I wake up every day and I do my best. Some days that's 150%. Other days, I rely on others just to make it to bedtime. That's ok, despite the self-help books saying otherwise. It isn't that I don't care. It isn't that I don't embrace life and all of its complexities and know all too well that we never know when our ticket is going to come up. Instead, it is acknowledging that some of the best things in life happen, when you just let them be.

I discovered I know less in my 30s than in my 20s. But this I know. At times I'm irritable and unbearable and cranky. I'm stubborn like my mother. I'm a bit odd. I crave meaningful connections but am an introvert. I love to try new things like roasting coffee and buying obscure plants that have no chance of survival (banana plants anyone) because it is fun to try and fail. I run races with mediocre times and battle the bulge, while still finding a way to love myself even though health blogs and beauty magazines tell me I'm obese. I tell bad jokes and most times people can't even tell if I'm joking. I'm inpatient. I'm independent. I'm loyal. The best thing is, all of this could change in a heartbeat because the thing I know most, is I'm a constant work-in-progress and that's what makes me, me. Enough so that I inked who I am on my wrist. But that's another story.

The truth is nothing lasts forever, not even a permanent multi-year cell phone family plan. Don't let fear get in the way of going for what you want. The reality is contracts are made to be broken. If nobody broke them, we wouldn't need it right? Better to be the gal that goes all in and changes her mind than never to take the chance.

At the time, the family plan seemed so daunting—so final. That it somehow took away my independence. The truth is, no sheet of paper has that power. Only I do. Decide, is he or isn't he worth it? If so, sign the document. Take the chance. I'm sorry if you end up in divorce court hating me. Just know that regret is an ugly beast, even uglier than the cell phone company coming after you because life took a nasty turn.

We all grow up being taught or learning that in order to be successful, our life needs to be a certain way. There are certain boxes you need to check along the way. That external forces will tell you if and when you are happy and if you've made it. I call bullshit.

The truth is, the sooner you mourn the loss of what others want you to be, the sooner you get to be you. The sooner you get to break the mold and decide for yourself what makes you happy. From there, nothing is off limits. I think of all the time I wasted trying to be a version of someone else's me and while it ultimately played a role in getting me here, I wish the road had been a bit smoother.

Cliché as it sounds, Wayne Gretzky had it right when he said, "you miss 100% of the shots you don't take." TAKE THE SHOT. Be you. Because at the end of the day, even if you miss it, at least you'll be left with someone you are proud to call you.

Chapter 7
Therapy

"There's nothing wrong with you," Chris said.

Time stopped. How is that even possible? A few months prior I started therapy to fix myself. Mom had been dead for over a decade. Despite graduating from college and landing my dream job, I had wasted my 20s away in a semi-destructive fashion. Perhaps I was just living my single days to their fullest. It is a fine line after all. Needless to say, something in my soul said I needed a change.

A year prior, I had quit my TV news job to become a Communications Specialist at a local environmental liberal arts college. It was a straight day job, with weekends and holidays off. The pace was more predictable and at times mundane. Come summer, the nearly empty campus and a generous vacation schedule allowed me to finally slow down and process the past decade. The journalist in me felt I was selling my soul to the dark side. My soul said if I didn't slow down, I was headed down a pathway that'd ultimately destroy me.

Brutal is the only way I can describe it. At times emotional. One night, out of boredom, I watched reruns of *The Real World* and drank an entire bottle of wine. Somewhere towards the bottom of the wine, I felt myself spiraling out of control. I feared becoming her. Looking at the cheap zinfandel, I wondered at what point my mom transitioned from social drinker to alcoholic. I'd never get to ask her. But in this moment, I felt uncomfortably close. I threw the bottle out.

I chatted with my primary medical doctor. She suggested therapy. I had run out of excuses and my insurance covered it. There was immediate availability at a clinic just 10-minutes from my apartment. I didn't know many folks in this new town I was now trying to make home so I figured I had nothing to lose. You only live once, right?

There was also Steve. The guy worth signing a cell phone family plan with. He was different than the other guys I'd dated. A keeper, some might say. Our conversation ran deep. I laughed a lot. He seemed emotionally available. The attraction was definitely real. Nearly a year into dating, a part of me wanted to run. To destroy things before he could break my heart. The other side of me, convinced I'd somehow mess this up because I was in fact a mess, wanted to do the work to ensure I'd get my happily ever after.

The perfectionist in me won out. I sign up for therapy convinced that a few deep conversations with a stranger would solve my grief, open my heart up and allow me to finally move past my mother's death. In my mind, it was time to accept my mother's death for what it was, close that chapter and start my life. Unfortunately, that's now how therapy works. Turns out, grief isn't easily wrapped up in a bow like that either.

Each week I'd find myself in a comfortable office sharing snippets of my past with a complete stranger. Conversations jumped from what life was like growing up to my career path to losing my mom and falling in love. It felt very disjointed. Not at all like in the movies. Chris rapidly scribbled notes down while I babbled on and on about all of the things I was trying to process. Occasionally he'd prompt me down another rabbit hole in which I'd bare another piece of my soul. Things I had never shared with anyone suddenly came spilling out – I was comforted by the knowledge that this man had taken an oath to never share my deep, inner secrets with anyone.

The more I talked, the more broken I felt. What a mess I am, I thought to myself. I jumped between moments of at least I'm taking action to fix myself to wondering if these questions were only reopening wounds that had long since healed. Regardless, it felt like action and after years of inaction. That somehow these conversations would lead to me being better. Fixed. A prettier, cleaned-up version of my best self. Therapy seemed magical in that moment, like the unsung hero who, if given the chance, could save anyone.

After 8 sessions or so, Chris explained he had enough information to diagnose me. Finally, a definition of this mess. Definition meant a solution. A pill. A treatment. A book to read. A way to move forward. To finally not be the motherless daughter whose life had turned messy but rather a woman ready to take control of her life and move forward.

Then he said the words that shook my world.

"There's nothing wrong with you."

Other words followed. A lot of them. An explanation about how grief is hard but that I was in fact processing it and it was complicated. How it was totally normal to be nervous about my relationship because I was ready to transition from living solo to inheriting a roommate. Moving in with Steve was a big deal for me because I had spent a decade alone. I had successfully changed careers, but a lot of my identity was tied to that career I just walked away from. Something about the 20s being a major transition in my life.

He also talked about how my mother dying may have dimmed me ever so slightly. That pre-mom, I was perhaps a bit more outgoing and probably felt like an extrovert. It was impossible for him to know if I used that as a façade to not address my mother's illness. Now I seem to be looking more inward. I was bit more reserved and at peace with that. Was that a result of my mother dying? Perhaps. My mom died at a very pivotal time in my life where I was figuring out who I was as a person. Not to mention, this would likely be one of the most defining moments of my life. This wasn't necessarily a bad thing. It just meant I had evolved as a human – something we all do throughout our lives.

"But, what does this mean," I asked.

In my head I am convinced he is wrong. He has to be because if he isn't wrong, that meant I was sentenced to this unsettling feeling for the rest of my life. That the random tsunami waves that knocked me on my ass would continue to be triggered by the most mundane unexpected moments forever moving forward. I would never be the carefree teenager who took chances and felt invincible. Instead, I'd always be on edge waiting for the next big ball of doom to drop.

"It means that without me finding a diagnosis, your insurance likely won't continue to pay for these sessions," he explained. "I want to be upfront about that. I still think there are things we could talk through but you really are fine. If I had to prescribe you anything, it'd be to go live your life. Move in with Steve and enjoy this new life you've built. You're ready."

I couldn't afford the out-of-pocket costs for these weekly talks.

It wasn't that I didn't have the money but I questioned the value of paying someone to tell me I was fine, when I knew I wasn't. I thought about getting a second opinion. I was convinced I could find another therapist who'd understand that I was not alright with being alright. I needed a definition of what was wrong with me and a pathway to getting better.

I left therapy and something happened that hadn't happened in a long time. I cried. For a very long time. I cried tears of rage for mom breaking me and abandoning me. Tears of loss flowed as I acknowledged that the person I was pre-mom was gone. Instead, I was stuck with this new version of myself forever. I cried until there was nothing left inside of me.

When the tears finally stopped my soul felt lighter. It'd take years to really understand, but in that moment, I began to realize that letting go of what was for what is meant space for new things. It meant exploring a new career that provided a more equalized balance between work and life. It meant time to start a side hustle writing. It meant giving my heart the space it needed to heal and eventually opening up to falling in love. It meant exploring the Northwoods of Wisconsin and rediscovering myself on the south shores of Lake Superior. It meant starting to understand the connections and triggers that caused those tsunami-sized waves of grief, but also making space to remember the good times with mom.

Don't get me wrong, I'd return to therapy many times in future years. Each time, I'd still ask the question, "am I broken?" Sometimes I wasn't as whole as I'd like. Other times, I just needed a neutral stranger to ask me tough questions and give me the space to process the answers out loud. To remind me that life is hard. That even on the easiest days, life can and will kick me on my ass. That said, I get to choose how I react, I get to decide what comes next in those moments.

Years later, I'd find myself in therapy again. I had lost all sense of self and dreamed of starting over. Now in my 40s, my career had stalled. I had grown tired of the Northwoods. Dad was sick. My relationship with my sisters was strained. I was a new mom. The honeymoon phase of my happily ever after had long since worn off. I was tired and felt life had become a series of mundane motions on repeat.

I wanted to run but I didn't know where to. Anywhere seemed better than the sticks of northern Wisconsin in the heart of winter. I just wanted a new start. I found myself once again in therapy, this time my therapist was an incredible lady who seemed to read my mind.

"If you could start over, what would you do," she asked.

"I don't know." But it doesn't matter, I thought to myself because I cannot.

She proceeded with some tough love. She reminded me that no choice is a choice. I was choosing to stay stuck by not doing anything. That inaction was in fact the action of doing nothing. I hated her in that moment.

"If you want to leave, leave. You have the knowledge and resources to do so. I wonder if that's really the heart of what's bothering you, though."

Steve would eventually join me in therapy and I'd share my frustrations. I'd share that I was living a life that felt unfulfilled because somewhere along the time, life had started happening to me instead of for me. I no longer felt in the driver seat of my own destiny.

A conversation ensued about choices. I was reminded that I chose this life. Hell, I fought for this life. I had chosen a career that provided a work-life balance that allowed me to be an incredible mother. I spent years struggling to become a mother, it didn't happen by accident. We had sought out our dream home on a beautiful, inland recreational lake, but that meant living in a very small place away from friends and family, but within driving distance of dad. These are choices I had made that lead me to this life I was living.

My therapist reminded me that this other life I dreamed of was void of making any choices. That if I wanted to start over, it'd mean making a choice about giving this all up. That's the thing about choices. Choices rarely come without change. Change rarely comes without losing something to gain something else.

I couldn't imagine my life without my family. I couldn't imagine working a 60-hour work week or not being home to say goodnight to my miniature me. I couldn't imagine a view without Moon Lake or the ability to be at my dad's bedside if he needs me. I couldn't imagine not having time to write, or garden, or read a good book on my deck. I couldn't imagine Christmas without snow and a massive 16-foot tree in my living room. I couldn't imagine not living next to endless green space or leasing chickens in the summer.

The what if game is a dangerous game if you allow it to consume your life. It is one thing to wonder what if, if that is followed by a big dream that you go pursue. It is entirely another telling yourself how wonderful life would be if you could live someone else's. I realize that now. Sometimes life hands me unexpected surprises completely out of my control. They knock me off my feet and make me angry at the world. But, for the most part, my life is the result of a series of choices I made, consciously and unconsciously, that I should embrace. If I don't, I should change them.

I went to therapy seeking a simple solution. A quick fix on what

I thought was broken. I left realizing (many years later) that being broken is what makes us human. It is what makes life beautiful and bold and messy and meaningful. I realize now a therapist can arm you with great tools but ultimately the only person who can do the work on you, is you.

It seems so simple but took me a long time to understand that nobody could fix me. That I was in fact doing what I needed to do to survive. Looking back, I genuinely believe things worked out the way they needed to for me. Delaying the full feelings of my mom's death until I was in a place to process them, helped me get to a place where I could start to understand the grieving process. To understand that even trivial moments could trigger memories of mom, and that was in fact ok. That, in fact, grief is not something you ever get over so you can go live your life. Rather, you learn to live with it forever.

Chapter 8
The Boy

I've spent a few chapters hinting around about the boy. I'll be frank. Steve23423 did not initially wow me. I had just moved across state lines to a small-town in northern Wisconsin. After 7-years of late-night drinking, destructive relationships and newsroom chaos, I needed a change. I had switched careers as part of my quest to take care of myself. It was now my lifeline to a new start.

I had a new job. I had listed my house in Duluth and was moving into a small, two-bedroom apartment just minutes from work. I'd work straight days with holidays off and a ton of vacation. It was a chance to start over. I knew I had to let parts of my old life go but I was scared. It was sheer and utter chaos and resulted in a lot of questioning but for the first time in years, I felt I was taking the steering wheel of my life back from a set of unrealistic expectations I had created.

The downside is I knew nobody. I was turning 27 and starting all over. I genuinely wanted a new start and I knew that meant a social circle that wasn't created on a barstool. It was 2005. Online social groups and connections weren't readily available in rural, northern Wisconsin. I didn't run at the time, enjoy the gym or think I was smart enough to join a book club. I was too broke to go back to school again. Online dating was gaining momentum and for those old enough to remember, Yahoo Dating was a thing. It seemed like the perfect place to meet some folks who could introduce me to some other folks, hence making a real-life social network in Wisconsin.

I put myself out there with the caveat that I was looking for friends. I had a lot of work to do on myself and dating was the last thing on my mind. At least that's what I told myself. As an average, plus-size woman wanting simple conversations and an occasional hike with someone stable (aka single and employed), the pickings were slim. After a few lackluster exchanges on the phone and email followed by a disastrous date, I was ready to throw in the towel.

Then, Steve23423 reached out to me. I checked his profile and other than discovering he was a single male, he disclosed nothing personal online. I like a good mystery and figured I had nothing to lose. Our initial email exchanges went much better. He was easy to write to and could formulate full sentence responses. Eventually, we exchanged phone numbers and then met for Chinese food and cheap beers.

I don't believe in love at first sight. Lust perhaps. But somewhere an hour into my beef and broccoli, I found myself oversharing stuff about myself with someone who seemed invested. Eventually, our conversation moved to the parking lot where we pretended to go separate ways but just kept talking. It was the perfect start for us.

Over the course of the next month, we'd navigate the complications of two independent individuals slowly falling for each other but fearful of getting hurt, only to hurt each other. For a moment, we went our separate ways and I imagine this story for many would end here. Ours didn't.

We couldn't stay apart. We pretended to be friends. That somehow by being just friends, everything would be easier. It wasn't. By summer, we were official. Something inside of me changed.

Steve made me want to be a better person—not for him but for myself. Much of my life was in disarray, despite outward appearances applying otherwise. I never slowed down to acknowledge the pain that came with losing my mom nearly a decade before. I had spent a decade drinking, having fun and making bad decisions to mask the turmoil inside. After years of delaying grief, I finally sought therapy. I slowly began rebuilding my life so that if and when we'd ever seal the deal, Steve might get a whole person.

The truth is, I needed to know that I'd be alright with or without him. I needed to address some demons and understand how my alcoholic mother was impacting my relationships with people, food, drinks and frankly anything else that passed my way. I had become a cut and run kind of gal. Open to everyone and everything as long as they didn't get too close and with the understanding or belief that anyone who came into my life would leave me.

Steve didn't leave. Don't get me wrong. We didn't have a perfect courtship and Steve is not Prince Charming. I do give credit where credit is due, though. He stayed when it would have been much easier to leave. In return, I did the work. Things changed after I met Steve. They didn't change because of him but I genuinely believe that timing is everything. If I had met Steve23423 a few months earlier, this story would have a very different ending.

Instead, we did all the things. I moved in. I bought furniture for his house and painted the walls a very permanent, dark blue. We moved again and bought a house together. We got a dog. He proposed. The wedding planning started. Then, the conversation no couple wants to have. Prenups and last names.

I didn't handle the prenup conversation well. We don't have one, partially because while I had done a lot of work on myself, I still felt I had a lot to prove. Somehow, a prenup implied I wasn't enough. That I wasn't bringing enough to the relationship so he had to protect his assets. The truth is he had probably googled "wedding checklist" and that was on there. He dropped it. The name thing, not so much.

I'm the youngest of three daughters. Both my sisters married and took their husband's last name. My aunts and uncles on my dad's side of the family did not have any children. I was the last remaining Erickson that could carry on my family's name. That meant something to me. I also don't do hyphenated names. It just seems like an unnecessary burden women carry for much of their lives and a waste of ink and space on signature cards. No offense to those who were brave enough to keep their name and take their spouses. I'm just an all or nothing kind of gal and hyphenating was a compromise I wasn't interested in making. My boss once told me that when compromising, often times both parties walk away feeling like they lost. What you need to find is common ground. I didn't know it at the time. I just knew the ultimatum in front of me, change my name or don't get married.

Neither option appealed to me. I was a 30-year-old grown ass adult and being an Erickson meant something to me. I did not want to give that piece of me up. But man, I wanted to become a Probst. I genuinely loved the man in front of me because he understood me. He gave me the space to be me. He supported my independence but was someone that no matter what scenario I placed myself in, I saw him by my side.

As our wedding approached, the nagging name thing hung over me like a dark cloud. Around me, it seemed like everyone I know was suddenly getting divorced. The former journalist and at times conspiracy theorist started to wonder if this was a sign from some divine intervention that this wasn't right. I started to ask people not why their marriage was successful, but instead why their marriages failed. It might sound morbid but the reality is about 50% of marriages in the United States will end in divorce or separation. To add to that, all the folks who remain married that shouldn't be, and it is no wonder I was curious and extremely skeptical. While my heart said to marry him and never look back, the practical Scandinavian in me screamed do the work. Check the boxes. Make sure this is what you want because this is forever.

I thought if I could anticipate why marriages fail, I could make my marriage different. Like I somehow had control over the person I was marrying and could make sure he never left me. I was young and naïve and I now understand that sometimes folks just grow and evolve and aren't meant to be. At the time, though, I wanted to enter my marriage with my eyes wide open, fully prepared and keep my last name.

The countdown to wedding day grew closer. The name thing lingered in the back of my mind as I tried to navigate the grief welling up due to wedding planning without my mom. Despite my sister's best efforts to do a day of trying on dresses, I found myself ultimately choosing my dress over my lunch break alone. That somehow by choosing to make the decision alone, I wouldn't notice the person missing.

By mid-summer, my in-decision was killing me. It had me questioning everything, trailing me like a dark cloud. I did what any good introvert would do. I told Steve I was throwing myself a solo bachelorette camping party on the North Shore of Minnesota. He didn't even question it.

I kicked off my wild adventure along the shores of Lake Superior with a 6-pack of Coors Light, s'more makings, Jack Link's jerky and a 6-inch sub. I built a fire near the shores of an inland river, pulled out my trusty journal and worked on a pros and cons list. Yep. I'm a list girl. I'm the girl that makes lists so she can check things off of them. I've been known to add something to my to do list after I've completed it, just so I can feel like I've accomplished things. I have training lists, bucket lists, work lists, goal lists, parenting lists, honey to do lists and pros and cons lists.

This is the Enneagram 1 in me. I like to believe that I make rational decisions based on the facts. (This despite me flipping a coin to decide my career path). The reality is, I'm a gut girl through and through. My gut rarely disappoints me and when it does, I at least know I did what I thought was best for me versus listening to someone else.

Somewhere at the tail end of that 6-pack, the pressure of the past few months implodes into a bridezilla meltdown that only great pines and aspens bared witness too. The anticipation of planning a perfect day is just too much because I knew nothing would make it perfect without mom. Don't get me wrong, this didn't stop me, in a moment of fairy tale longing, to purchase an oversized Cinderella ballgown and extra-large crinoline because I deserved to have my princess moment. The problem is I'm not a princess and my queen is dead.

I went to bed depleted, a little drunk and on a serious sugar-high from overindulging in extra sweet, double Hershey stacked, multi-marshmallow s'mores. I woke up extra early and stumbled down to the river to splash some cool water on my face. I sat by the banks knowing that.

What do I really want? I find myself asking. Is this over-the-top research and angst about my name a sign I'm not ready to get married. Or, is it just me being overly cautious with my heart? Is this an attempt to cut and run so that he cannot cut and run on me? Do I think for even a second that by somehow marrying Steve I am giving up the heart of who I am? Is that why the name thing bothers me so? Every time I struggle with these questions, the same answers came back to me. When I look into my future, there isn't a moment I could think of where I'd be better off without him than with him. The gut girl wins, and my cold feet disappear.

A few months later, Steve and I would say I do before a retired judge. I, with my oversized body stuffed into that princess gown. My father and Steve in tuxedos. A blustering storm rolling in off Lake Superior. Family and friends surrounded us, unable to hear the words but standing witness to two people just trying to figure it out together. By nightfall, our lakeside overlook would be surrounded by a pea-soup thick fog.

Later, during the father-daughter dance, my dad would simply ask me, "does he make you happy?"

"Yes."

"Then I'm happy for you."

Tender moments like this book ended with endless laughter and lots of dancing created a memorable night I will never forget. It also marked another major milestone without my mom. I missed her reassurance and tough love wisdom. Had she been here, I know when my doubts started, she simply would have said, *do you love him? If so, then marry him. If you don't, don't marry him.* Decisiveness was her specialty.

I missed having her see me try on dresses and taste test cakes and watch me walk down the makeshift aisle as the man she loved gave me away. It would have been a full circle moment. I wish more than anything she could have been there. But what'd I tell myself now is it was ok that today was about so much more than her.

The truth is, I shed very few tears on my wedding day. Ceremony thoughts included, God I'm lucky, I hope it doesn't start raining, and I wish I had done more upper body work-outs because I can feel my backfat hanging out of the top of my dress. Two of my best friend's would keep my mom's presence alive, first with an Elizabeth Barrett Browning reading during the ceremony and later a toast mentioning those we love missing. In both cases the loss bubbled to the surface but didn't stick around.

I don't know why. Perhaps it was because this day wasn't about losing my name or the people missing at my table. Instead, I focused on what I gained. It doesn't diminish one's loss but I wish I hadn't punished myself so much for experiencing joy. The truth is, you get to have both if you choose to. Emotional multi-tasking at its finest. It is a treasure we should never take for granted.

Steve and I didn't become one when we got married. We didn't even merge bank accounts. Instead, we made a commitment to be there for each other in good times and bad. To hold each other accountable and encourage us to reach our potential as two individuals committed to sharing a life together.

For those wondering, I took his name. It marks a promise I made to him that I'll stay by his side through thick and thin, as long as he holds up his end of the bargain. It isn't a prenup but it is a promise that I plan to keep.

Choosing Probst didn't mean losing Erickson, though. It isn't uncommon to hear, that's the Erickson in her coming out. I often tell stories to my son Jake about the Erickson side of his genes, enough so that at one point, he demanded to change his name. Turns out, it doesn't take a sheet of paper to remember your roots.

The truth is marriage is not a fairy tale and I'm not some princess. The greatest love stories of all time are often framed in loss. Can we say *The Notebook* and *Romeo and Juliet*? Real relationships are hard. They take commitment, conversation, common ground, humility and lots of I'm sorry. They also mean giving up a small piece of who you are to become a part of something greater. Someday this relationship on earth will end. I'm not sure who will outlive who but if it is me, despite how difficult the loss will be, I will remain forever grateful to Yahoo for bringing Steve23423 into my life.

Chapter 9
Faith

I've always viewed religion through a lens of skepticism and curiosity. Growing up, I was skeptical about some of the facades that were framed to me as faith. I was, what I'd consider, a lazy Lutheran. I religiously attended Sunday school and confirmation and sat with my friends in the back pews taking notes during the sermon which demonstrated we were listening—also known as attendance. (So much for faith).

I listened to these lessons of forgiveness, redemption, limitless love and protection while watching my mother slowly die at home. At times I leaned hard into the message of hope. At other times, I cursed a God I didn't understand.

In middle school, I started attending my best friend's church youth program. It was filled with ski trips, bowling, summer adventures to amusement parks and river tubing and my high school crush willing to hold my hand during a wild game of Romans and Christians. In the summer, we'd travel cross-country in a van sleeping on church floors and perform a contemporary Christian musical. It was my window to the world.

The program provided a framework for my faith. One year in particular, our musical politely called out the hypocrisy found within the church walls. Gossip, judgement, holding grudges—these were all too familiar feelings I understood. But somehow, the pastor added perspective to these emotions. The musical ended with a new message of hope. A message that I'd carry with me for years.

My parents were casual church goers. They'd listen to our out-of-tune church programs and ensure we were baptized, confirmed, and exposed to God. Holiday services were also a given. Come Christmas Eve and Easter, we'd pack ourselves in like sardines with the rest of the lazy Lutherans in the back on stage left.

Looking back, I still recall the emotions swelling up inside of me as hundreds came together to sing Silent Night by candlelight. Sometimes, I'd end up squished between my two sisters. While they often fought, they always found a way to bond when torturing me. I can still feel the hot wax dripping on my legs as they "accidentally" tilted their candles my way.

One time when my dad was ill, the local hospital chaplain stopped by. After making small talk, he posed a simple question to my father.

"Would you like to pray?"

My father nodded yes.

I wasn't in the mood but I quietly lowered my head and respected my father's wishes. As my father closed his eyes and listened to this stranger's prayer, I wondered what was going through his mind.

Afterwards, I asked what seems obvious, "do you even believe in God?"

"Of course. Why would you think I don't," he says with the conviction of a father who is ending a conversation. I'm annoyed in that moment so I ignore the hint.

"Let's see, maybe because I've never seen you pray or go to church unless you had to."

"I don't need church to believe in God," he said.

It struck me then that for all the years I had taken care of my dad, I knew very little about him or his faith. Thinking about it, though, it started to make sense that he was a man of God. My father's faith helped him navigate the love of his life battle with addiction. Even in her darkest moments, he never left. Once sober, they had a second chance. God had a different plan. At sixteen months sober, my mom died. Dad stood there holding her hand. Later, it'd be the same faith that helped him decide in a single moment to quit drinking and smoking. He'd remain sober and smoke free until the day he died. Sure, he didn't flaunt his faith by teaching Sunday School or sitting front and center for weekly sermons. Did he really need to, though?

This unwavering commitment did not extend to me. My relationship with God is much more tenuous. It's a bit fair weathered at times. Until I met Kendra. Kendra believed in my writing before I did. The Travel Editor at *Midwest Living Magazine*, I once queried her with a mediocre story idea. She politely declined but enjoyed my writing sample. She gave me a shot to do some travel scouting.

I was newly married and this was my dream side hustle. I'm a frugal traveler so to travel on someone else's dime and share my experiences was priceless. Even more priceless is the mentorship that ensued.

Over the course of 5-years we became writing buddies. She was candid in her criticism of my writing style and kept things real when I told her about my dreams of becoming a full-time writer. She walked that fine line of coach, mentor and at times realist. More than once, her emails would be packed with real-talk that helped me stay on course both in writing and my career.

At one point, Steve and I struggled to conceive. We went the adoption route. While we sat in the endless waiting game wondering if and when we'd ever get chosen, Kendra was quick to pick me up. She, too, had adopted and understood the emotional roller coaster that comes with it. Somewhere along the way, her cats ended up moving from her place in Des Moines, Iowa to my home in Iron River, Wisconsin.

It seemed logical at the time. The cats needed to be relocated because her son had developed allergies. I had space and a few pets so figured, why not? Chickpea and Mischief would quickly become a foundational component of the Probst household. Geriatric and extremely lazy, they rarely wreaked havoc in the house. Right until Chickpea ran away from home. Chickpea was dainty and 100 percent an indoor cat. Occasionally she'd sneak out to eat grass a few feet off the deck, but she'd quickly be scooped up or back at the door begging to come in.

This time she disappeared altogether. After a day or two, I began to fear the worst. We live on a dead-end street but it is just a block off a busy county highway. Predators, like foxes, are regularly spotted on our streets. Given her agile nature and age, the cards were stacked against her. We created some flyers and posted them on social media. Fearful that Kendra would see it there first, I reached out to share the bad news.

Later that day, she let me know that she had sent prayers to St. Anthony, the patron saint of lost things. As someone who is not Catholic, I giggled at the notion that faith would be involved in my missing cat. The next day a neighbor down the street called to let us know they had Chickpea. She had been found in a nearby campground and was keeping the cat until she figured out where it belonged.

Coincidence, perhaps. The story repeated itself a few years later when Mischief escaped our house. (I swear we are good pet owners but also human). Mischief would be gone for 5-days before we notified Kendra. I thought for sure he was a goner. The next day, a lady known for her love of cats would be called to trap an unruly black cat on the other side of town – about 2-miles away. An acquaintance of ours, she immediately recognized the gnarled up black furball as Mischief. He was home before dinner, hangry and disheveled but completely fine.

Coincidence again? Perhaps. But this story has an even more unusual ending. Kendra would go on to be diagnosed with multiple sclerosis and later leukemia. Over a series of a few years, I watched in awe as Kendra defied death more times than I can count. Each time, she battled with humor, strength and grace.

Grace is not a word that frequented my vocabulary back then. Kendra changed that. On a Duluth trip during the height of her illness, she asked me to join her for breakfast at the Duluth Grill. Her only request – some Bayfield apples. Over breakfast, we made small talk. She asked about my future as a writer. She continued to mentor and advise me, even as she fought for her life. At the time, I tried to deny the reality of what was happening. Kendra, always the editor, reminded me this would likely be the last time we connected over coffee. She was not one to leave things left unsaid. She encouraged me to continue writing and exploring and to be fearless in my faith—whatever that might look like for me.

Kendra's commitment to faith astounded me. She did not for a single second question God in this horrific dilemma. I have to believe that if we were close, I would have seen moments of doubt. But as I watched her story continue to unfold via social media and the occasional letter, I couldn't help but be in awe of her unrelenting trust in a power higher than us.

At just 46, she'd breath her last breath. Her final social post reminded friends and family that she had left nothing unsaid and to remember that we'd see her on the other side, "where God's holy hand will cradle us all in strength and goodness."

I still question my faith. It isn't that I don't believe in something. I just don't believe that something owes me anything. That somehow, things will always work out for me. I believe I need to show up and do the work and only then will I see the results. There are no handouts. That said, I am starting to understand that the world is bigger than I and that someone much smarter than I, is looking out for me.

After losing my mom, I wanted to see angels. I cannot explain why. Perhaps it is an attempt to soften the heartache that comes with losing the single most influential person in my life. Or, it is the unexplainable moments where her presence feels so real that I hear her speaking into my head. I've come to accept in these moments that perhaps the hardest part of faith is believing what you feel, even though everything you can prove says it is not. I know I could find some logical explanation for why I'm hearing her voice or feeling her presence in certain situations. I find myself asking why do I continue to do that? If faith brings me comfort during difficult times, then why question it? Why not embrace it? Better yet, why try to take that away from someone else or prove to them that their faith is grounded in nothing more than their heart?

When my father died, the presence of angels seemed stronger. Perhaps I was more open to feeling his presence—a desire to believe he could see my son playing basketball or hitting his first homerun in baseball. Or, in allowing myself space to experience joy and sorrow, it was easier to open up my heart and recognize that my parents continue to live on in and around me. I bear witness to that almost every day when I allow myself to.

I question my faith more than ever, but feel closer to a higher power than ever before. I sense the awe and wonder of something, someone out there watching out for me and those I love. It is a reassuring feeling in an uncertain time that I cannot explain, other than to say I am so glad I have opened up my heart and mind to that which I don't understand or cannot prove or disprove.

The truth is, when I let go of needing to believe I understand the universe and all of its workings, it allowed my faith to evolve without judgement or a rush to figure it all out. Faith isn't all or nothing, any more than weight loss. Asking questions makes me curious, not a non-believer. Faith is personal, not familial. Just because I grew up in one religion, doesn't mean this cannot evolve and change over time. It doesn't mean I've quit believing, but instead I had quit being a blind believer. I was baptized before I could speak or think. In many ways, this is a blessing. But how incredibly more meaningful as I age to base my faith on what I've taken time to question and accept what I can never fully understand.

Chapter 10
The Adoption

"Are you sitting down?"

"Of course," my husband and I anxiously replied from a mostly empty parking lot in-between our work places. A million thoughts raced through my mind.

Is the baby, ok?

When do we get to see him?

Why aren't we already heading south?

Did something happen with our paperwork?

"I have an update for you," the social worker said, speaking slower than usual. "The baby was born yesterday and is doing well, as-is mom."

"Should we be there? How soon should we head down," I asked.

We wait for what feels like eternity before she continues.

"Mom is having second thoughts. It started towards the end of her pregnancy and at this point she isn't sure she wants to move forward. At this point, she'd prefer you not go to the hospital as planncd."

The social worker continued talking but I don't understand another word she says. Second thoughts are to be expected. After all, mom said she loved the baby but had no desire to be a parent so it seemed appropriate that she might be having doubts now that the day is here. But, why wouldn't we be by her side?

I hear my husband ask, "so how sure is sure? Is there any chance she'll change her mind in this situation?"

"They rarely change their minds. I'm afraid her decision is likely final," the social worker said.

I make a final hail marry attempt to put things back together.

"Did she say why? Can we speak to her? Maybe she's just having doubts."

"She's asked to not speak to you guys and for you to respect her privacy."

With that, our adoption journey ends. We would never meet Sullivan Probst. Sully for short. But I loved him anyway. Intense pain ensues while I slowly processed what would never come to fruition.

We began our adoption journey after several years of failed attempts at getting pregnant the good old-fashioned way. We had committed to multiple appointments to ensure our parts were in working order and even started down the long and daunting journey of fertility treatment.

We thought adoption was a noble alternative. That perhaps we could provide a child with a kind, loving, stable environment in a world where so many kids go without. We were excited. Then anxious. Then overwhelmed.

The paperwork is daunting. The cost is exorbitant. The questions are intrusive. At one point, my husband and I find ourselves taking a marriage counseling assessment.

"What if we fail?" I joked with our social worker.

"It isn't a pass-fail test, just an opportunity to strengthen your relationship," she explained.

Yet, this same woman would soon come to our home to complete a home study. To ensure that our house was baby proofed, even though we had no baby. To verify proof of pet vaccinations, and that we had a daycare slot firmly secured at a licensed daycare facility. She'd ask us about our values, our faith and judge our worthiness of parenting. She would slowly walk through our house making small talk, trying to ease our fears, as we await word if we'll pass our home study. We do. A single approval and I'm somehow deemed worthy of being a parent.

Next, there is the scrapbook. Each couple wanting to adopt creates a handmade scrapbook for expecting moms to browse. This is how they decide who they want to interview. In other words, the fate of my future as a mother relies on my scrapbooking skills. I am not a scrapbooker. I hate crafts. Yet, I find myself up to my elbows in glitter, glue and glossy photos attempting to sell our life story to a complete stranger. Our letter to mom is heartfelt. Our decision to include a photo of our dog on the cover is a bit more calculated. Our social worker explained that there are dog people that are immediately drawn to covers with animals and that is a common, positive differentiator for a mom going through up to 60 books to find a match.

The marketer in me can't help but wonder what our selling point is. Is it our high-quality school district or lakeshore home? Perhaps our Chevy Chase style holidays and love of the outdoors. Our rural versus urban setting. Or, our longing to love someone so much it hurts. I somehow finish the project and the waiting begins.

Time and time again our book is picked from the pile only to be discarded when it came time for interviews. Then, 6-months in we get the call. A woman in her 40s is pregnant. The guy is married to someone else and has a son. He, in his own words, has no desire to be a dad again. She is equally determined not to be a mother. Losing track of time, she went to abort the baby only to find out she was too far along. As time went on, she grew fonder of the child growing inside of her – enough so that she quit smoking - but knew she didn't want to be a mother.

At least that's the story they told us during a supervised social worker visit on their home turf. At 8-months pregnant, the clock was ticking. We did our best to be our authentic selves knowing that the stakes were high during this meeting.

Conversation flowed. Soon we were laughing and telling stories about our families. After they leave the room, we exhale for the first time in an hour. A little crack of hope seeps into my heart. Perhaps this will work. I allow myself to believe.

The social worker joins us. Asks us our thoughts on the interview. We are overly eager and ready to accept nearly any terms to make this happen. The magic words are spoken.

"If you are still interested, the couple has decided they'd like to move forward with you in the adoption process."

My heart bursts.

"Yes!"

A few weeks later we'd meet for lunch at a family café about an hour south of her home. Here, we'd walk the line of getting to know each other a little better while also plotting out a plan. There is much to discuss over burgers.

Are we doing an open adoption?

Will the birth parents have the option to visit?

Will Sully know his birth parents?

How often will we exchange photos? Allow for visits?

Handle holidays?

In our haste to make things easy, we throw nearly every bound-ary out the window. I open myself to nearly anything to ensure this happens. I figure somehow, it'll all work out.

We part ways in the parking lot snapping a few photos of each other. We realize the next time we'll see each other we'll be at the hospital. We hug.

It feels right.

Right until it doesn't. A few weeks later, I notice mom is distant. A little less responsive. The over analyzer in me contacts our social worker concerned things are going to fall apart. She reassures me this is one of the cleanest cut adoption cases she's ever seen. With decades of experience, I believe her. I go all in. She suggests that perhaps Mom is just pulling back a bit. That she's maybe overwhelmed and I should just trust the process.

Mom finally emails me and assured me all is well. Dad is just crabby and there's a bit of tension but we're full steam ahead. I drop my guard more.

My friends, while nervous this could still fall apart, host a beautiful shower. The buttercream frosted carrot cake topped with the words *Welcome Transition* acknowledge the world I'm about to enter. I find myself with just a few weeks to assemble a baby room and adjust to the idea of being a mother. I resigned from the committees, notified my employer and worked ahead on my freelance. I read baby books and folded onesies and stocked up on diapers. I researched homemade baby food making.

In an instant, the transition is over. No additional planning needed. In the immediate aftermath, I use process to numb my mind. I send sterile emails and updates to those I might see in the next few weeks. I pack up the nursery and shut the door. I plan a date at a local County Fair to distract my broken heart. I let my employer know I'll be back at work in a few days, hoping work will consume me. I am completely numb.

Weeks later, our social worker would ask if we were ready to go back in the pool. To climb back on the saddle and go again. I couldn't fathom going again when we had no closure on the son we lost.

I asked the social worker if birth moms who changed their mind ever did phone calls explaining their decision – a conversation that I hoped might bring me closure. She discouraged it but said she'd ask. A few days later, closure came in the form of another blow.

"The mom doesn't feel she owes you an explanation. She does not want to speak to you."

Succinct and to the point. But it's hard to swallow. Just weeks before, we were welcoming mom into our home and figuring out how to incorporate a lifetime of unconventional holidays out so that if nothing else, baby Sully would always know he was loved unconditionally. Now, I'm forced to reckon with a loss I'll never understand.

Down and out, I sought one last reassurance. "He'll be ok right? The fact that she kept him must mean she really loves him," I asked the social worker.

Perhaps it was her tenure or a recent case that was on her mind, but she pauses before explaining that in her experience, the moms that could be great mothers often go through with the adoption while the ones who probably aren't ready are the ones that often change their mind. I don't know if that's true. I hope not. As a mother now, I understand the unexplainable bond between mother and son and why it would have been so difficult. At the time, I just saw red.

I do my best to resume daily living. I go through the motions – eat, sleep, work, repeat. I make small talk with people and assure them I'm fine. I continue training for a half-marathon. Time keeps moving. I assume everyone knows of my loss. Many do not. After all, why would they? I run into a casual acquaintance at the library nearly a month after we received the news.

"How's motherhood treating you," she asked.

"It isn't," I said, attempting to explain the situation when the damn of tears breaks. I'm immediately ashamed but once it starts, I cannot make it stop. To me, I feel I've ripped open a dam of pain. Just a few alligator-sized tears escape my eyes.

A raw and awkward moment between two nearly strangers. Yet, I find this near stranger holding my pain for me. I exhale and regain my composure. We make small talk, a casual reference to the weather, and how things are going for the local library, a board that once consumed my life. For a moment, life almost seems normal. A weight is lifted. I start to believe that maybe someday the numbness will go away.

Walking away, I suddenly find intense anger bubbling up inside of me. I'm angry at mom – not so much for changing her mind but for disregarding our family like yesterday's trash. A family that had went 100% in and shared our life and dreams and hopes for this unborn baby. I wanted a baby badly and that she was willing to abort if the State had let her. I'm fearful for what lies ahead for Sully and scared that I'll never get to be a mom. These are harsh thoughts built out of loss but a necessary evil for me to move forward in this moment.

I go home and journal. That's what a writer does. I scroll mindlessly on social media welcoming the distraction of happy people living their lives. Someday I'll get back to that, I think to myself. I allow just a hint of hope that by letting the pain in, perhaps joy will follow. Then I see it. A short essay contest for an all-expenses trip to a local Lake Superior weekend retreat called Girl's Gone North.

The deadline is today. They ask for just 250 words about why you and your girlfriends deserve a weekend away. I channel my sadness into the only thing I know. Hope. I hope that someday I'll be happy again. That a weekend away with my tribe may mend my broken heart. I somehow win.

Several months later my girlfriends and I gather for a weekend of love and laughter. A makeover is part of the prize, which as a tomboy, is hilarious. I drink a bit too much wine and shed a few tears on the greatest of great lakes – Lake Superior.

The ebb and flow of happiness and grief reminds me that I am strong. There will always be a special place for Sully in my heart but my heart is big enough to consider going back into the adoption pool. I reckon with the reality that I'll never get closure from Sully's parents. That perhaps closure isn't a real thing but a marketing ploy that plays out in an attempt to mark the beginning, middle and end of grief.

I realize that closing the book on Sully would break my heart. It'd somehow suggest that time erases all that Sully represents – my desire to be a mother. My desire to love someone unconditionally. I commit to holding space for loss and love in my heart.

I return to work on Monday not a changed woman but a woman with hope restored in humanity. A woman who believes her tribe can help carry her through some of the darkest months since losing my mom many moons ago and now having that dream of becoming one taken away as well. Many adoption stories end in heartbreak – it is just a matter of whose heart is broken. But occasionally there is a happy ending.

Somehow post grief, my husband and I create Jacob William Probst or Jake for short. On Sully's first birthday, my dream of motherhood is fulfilled when I give birth to my son.

Time keeps moving. Random, unexpected moments still leave me wondering about Sully. I sometimes find myself wondering what if and think to myself how crazy it would be if Jake had a brother. That wondering leads me to send a letter to mom when Jake's a few years old. I share our good news and then ask the simple question, how's he doing?

As I hit send, I believe she'll respond with a quick update and congratulations. After all, years had passed and we'd respected her wishes. It seems like a simple bookend – that word closure once again prying its way into my life. She never responds.

The sheer act of asking put my mind at rest. To know I had allowed myself to love, grieve and live simultaneously. I left no words unsaid and left a door open, should mom ever want to reach out. I know I'd want that opening if the situation were reversed. I also know that the likelihood is slim to none. As hard as that is to accept, I'm ok with that.

The thing is, much in life one cannot control. A popular self-help guru always says attitude and effort are the only things you control. Choosing to hold anger towards mom only hurt me. It held me back from being me. Mom successfully delayed my dream of motherhood but I wasn't willing to give up being me as well.

I'll never understand or forget mom's refusal for a simple conversation. I did, though, manage to forgive myself for the anger I held on to as part of my effort to avoid the void in my heart named Sully. I realize that when you forgive yourself, space opens up for what's next. You suddenly don't feel quite as stuck. Sure, I still felt hurt, but there was movement towards something else.

When the adoption failed, there was no funeral. There was no closure or moment to grieve. It was hard to know what to grieve. After all, the child didn't die. To find comfort, I did my best to put baby first and believe that if mom decided she wanted to be a mother, it made sense for them to stay together. In doing so, I never acknowledged my grief. I didn't understand why I was hazy and emotionally depleted in the days that followed. Instead, I was frustrated with myself for not being better prepared for what happened. I couldn't help but wonder how the state deemed me ready to be a parent, but this stranger stripped me of my right to be a mother.

We were surrounded by love and by people with the best intentions. In their mind, our hearts were broken but we could be chosen again in a heartbeat if we just put ourselves back in the pool. It was tragic but not a real tragedy. I frankly agreed with them, making the process even more difficult. It'd be months before I was ready to say good-bye to Sully. I imagine that parting letter to mom was my way of moving forward. To processing and recognizing I'd never know what happened and that had to be ok. I still find myself wondering how he's doing and pray he's safe. I did however quit living in the moment where I blamed myself believing that if I had just done something different, the outcome would be different. Perhaps this is bargaining. Or just trying to justify the unjustifiable.

The truth is loss is worthy of your attention. Comparing your loss to others and trying to convince yourself that somehow your loss isn't worthy of grieving because it isn't bad enough is dangerous. Your loss is worthy. It demands space and attention regardless of any unrealistic expectation of other people's opinions you are putting on yourself. Grief if grief. It doesn't go away. No matter how hard you try to rush through it, justify it or wish it away, it will always find you.

Chapter 11
The Valentine

"I hope you take a long walk off a short pier."

To say our friendship started off unconventional would be an understatement. Instead, it was this statement penned on a 4th grade Valentine that began a lifelong friendship that's always been grounded in brutal honesty.

I honestly don't why I penned that Valentine to Cara with such rage. But when I reached out to her to verify this infamous card, she reminded me that Valentine went on to call her a bitch, and that I had a way with words that were now, nearly 35-years later paying off.

I was a pretty rotten human back then.

Seriously. Think back to your younger days. I'm sure there are a few not-so-great moments in your memory chest that you wish you could do over knowing what you know now. Or maybe you were better than me? All I know is this Valentine's Day card was nothing compared to some of the drama that ensued around me growing up as I attempted to win at any cost. What's crazy is that the recipient of this card was often a willing participant in this insanity. A gal who willingly requested a seat on my crazy train.

Despite being extremely boy crazy from a young age, my first kiss didn't come until my early teens. Why is this relevant in regards to my friendship with Cara? Because that kiss should have been hers.

My parents allowed me to bring a friend camping for a week at the height of summer. We had one goal – to attach ourselves to some boys. We were immediately successful. The boys were sweet. Innocent. Kind. We enjoyed a week of bike rides, playing catch, attending nature shows and hanging out at the beach. We were the perfect foursome. There was one problem. They wouldn't kiss us. We were solidly in the friend zone from day one, not to mention I think they were late bloomers. Always the competitive one, I was determined to leave that trip a changed woman.

The last night, we saw an older boy having a bonfire on the beach by himself. We chatted him up. He told us to come back later. We promised we would. We pretended to sleep and later snuck out of our tent and scrambled down to the beach. We thought we were so cool sneaking out on our own only to hear my mother mutter, "keep it down girls and be sure to let us know when you get back."

I imagine our little rendezvous seemed harmless and my parents figured the mosquitos would drive us back to the safety of our tent within the hour. If only they knew.

We approached the mysterious boy on the beach. It was clear Cara was interested. It was clear he was interested back. Let's be honest – Cara was the funny, outgoing one. I, the moody, serious one. We complimented each other well but a part of me always wished I was a bit more carefree like Cara.

Watching them on the beach, I was jealous. While an introvert,

I'm also competitive. The competitive side of me won even though Cara wasn't competing. I made a move and somehow scored my first kiss. It was anything but magical and while victorious, the victory seemed hollow. Eventually, Cara grew tired of my escapade and returned to our campsite. There, my parents were patiently waiting to make sure we made it home safely. When she arrived without me, hell hath no fury. My evening quickly came to an end.

The next morning, I saw the boy swimming. I approached him to say goodbye and he did a mad dash sprint to his campsite to hide from me. He pretended not to see me. As I approached the campsite (yes, I am that stupid or determined, it is a fine line), his father tried to tell me he had already left. Cara couldn't help but laugh at the irony of the entire event. I tell you, karma's a bitch sometimes. In hindsight, if the tables were turned, I doubt Cara would have done the same. In fact, I know she wouldn't because Lord knows she had the opportunity.

A few months later, she'd prove that point by playing wingman for me. A quick introduction and urging me to take a chance secured me a kiss with my crush on the roof of her church while playing Romans and Christians during Sunday Youth Group. It was meaningful, magical and the start to a year-long crush. A night I'll never forget thanks to her. A true testament to a friend who only wants what's best for you, even if you don't deserve it.

Similar situations would play out over the course of decades. This incredible human would come to experience the best and worst of me on endless occasions. We were inseparable, often times called sisters due to our similar Scandinavian looks. At times, I think we knew each other and each other's secrets better than we knew ourselves.

As high school approached, our interests shifted. Our circle of friends broadened. Our time together often reflected circumstances outside of our control. Jobs, hobbies, boyfriends, family drama, schoolwork and the other complexities of teenage life consumed us.

Perusing middle and high school journals are painful. A bad after-school special of unnecessary drama and anger often times directed toward those I cared about most. It is safe to say if I had invested a $20 every-time I told Cara I was mad at her, I'd certainly be retired by now.

At some point, we slowly outgrew each other. There was no pivotal moment where we quit being friends. Where I hurt her to the point of no return or she finally realized she deserved friends better than me. Instead, life happened. I moved away, at first 20-minutes, and later over an hour. She got married and had kids while I was busy drinking my 20s away. Our hobbies and interests changed. We grew up and grew apart but share a foundation that'll never crack. We remain friends to this day, but it is different. As it should be. We're different people but still share decades of memories and only the best for each other. We recently got together for coffee and conversation flowed for hours, even though it had been years since we'd seen each other in person. Friends like this are rare. To be cherished for sure.

The evolution of this friendship is representative of so many friendships that have ebbed and flowed over the years of my life. I've been blessed with countless girlfriends who show up in my life at the most unexpected but necessary times. These unexpected gifts have become a series of Angels that I will never take for granted.

When I say Angels, I'm not talking about the kind you see in movies or church ceilings. You know the ones I'm talking about. The kind with wings who flit in and out of your life and provide great wisdom from above. The kind that never get their hands dirty. The ones who are all-knowing and guide you through life. Those ones might exist as well. What I'm talking about, though, are the ones that sit in the muck with you. The ones that when things get dark, offer you a bottle of tequila, a full-fat, double whip latte, a hike in the woods, a pedicure or all four depending on the day. The kind that laughs with you until you pee your pants and don't judge your tears. Who understand your mood swings and your introverted tendencies. The ones who don't even question you when your mouth opens, and unfiltered thoughts come pouring out that nobody ever should hear. The ones who encourage your crazy hopes and dreams, while at the same time keeping you in-check when you get a little too big for your britches. These are the Angels that make life worth living.

Cara was the first of many angels in my life. When I look back on the moments in my life that matter – she's always been there. Good or bad, it doesn't matter. She just keeps showing up. A glutton for punishment I suppose. I can only hope she's gained something out of this lifetime of ups and downs I've thrown her way.

I think we all have a few wishful do-over moments with friends. Many of those land with Cara. But as any friend of mine will attest, there is plenty more to go around. There's an infamous middle school ketchup fight. A dear friend who I blasted as a new mom because I didn't understand why she was too busy to hang out with me (I was still living out my single years). And perhaps my lowest moment, slapping a girl across the face over a boy (that didn't even like me). While I am an introvert, I am a woman of many words when it comes to shooting off an email or Facebook message—many of which I have come to regret and many of which were written because I misinterpreted someone's life circumstance and made it about me. I refrain from sending these now – but ask my husband. He's been the recipient of a few over the years. It is a hard habit to crack.

Dan Pink recently wrote a book all about regrets. In it, he talks about the only people who don't have regrets are children, sociopaths, or those struggling from a stroke. What matters is what one does with their regrets. This doesn't mean that you cannot regret something and learn from it—in fact that's what you should do. It does mean that none of us carry a magic 8 ball. That sometimes we make mistakes or wish we could take something back. It is called being human. What does matter is what we do armed with this new information.

I hope I am a better friend today than in 4th grade. Yes, I know the bar is low but bear with me. I try my best to show up for the Angels in my life while at the same time recognizing that sometimes, someone comes into your life at the right moment, only to leave it the next. It doesn't mean they won't be back, often times in the moment you need them most. It also isn't a reflection of you – that somehow you weren't good enough. It is often just a reflection of the circumstances. It was a tough lesson to learn but my life is much richer because of it. Life is funny that way.

Social media has skewed our understanding of friendships on many levels. It keeps us connected to so many people on a surface level. It is comforting and at times joyful to see the people you once considered your closest friends succeeding in life. It helps you realize how similar to many of us are—how many of my mom friends struggle to get their kids to wear pants or don't find it at all odd when you brag about your kid winning a basketball game at 8 like he just signed for the NBA. There are universal emotions—love, grief, anger, frustration, exhaustion—that provide comfort in a digital space, if even for a moment.

I appreciate social media for these connections, and am careful to avoid comparing my life to these updates. My energy goes towards my real-life Angels, though. I've looked very closely at those who get a seat at the table in my life – the people I turn to for wisdom, strength, courage, and conversations. I go on wild adventures with people I admire and spend evenings sipping cocktails locked in deep conversation. Rarely will you see me making small talk at a bar with strangers—but I have found my curiosity to understand people at a deeper level resulting in some incredibly meaningful relationships.

Sometimes losing a friend or letting go of a friendship that no longer serves you makes space for new friends. It is a kind way to leave an opening for a reconnection in a future season of life. It doesn't make it easier, but real friendships take work. They take patience, kindness, empathy, understanding and a lot of grace. Just ask Cara, who still manages to giggle about the 4th grader who weaseled her way into her life by being anything but normal.

Truth is intentionality matters. It takes time, energy and effort to cultivate new friendships. Trust and boundaries, respect and commonality are critical. Much goes into those first few tender months of getting to know each other. Check your ego and your intentions. Be honest and real. Vulnerable when necessary. You'll soon find yourself surrounded by incredible people that will catch you when you fall, check your attitude, and nudge you ahead when needed. Last but not least, when you fuck up, own it. Let the record show Cara, the only bitch in 4th grade was me.

Chapter 12
I Am Not a Runner

I never considered myself a runner. A tomboy, perhaps, but a pudgy one. Growing up, I was extremely active. I spent my days riding my Huffy 10 speed bike to town so I could chase boys and swim at the local pool. I played basketball and softball. I loved a good hike in the woods. Despite this activity, I was a hearty, big boned Scandinavian who never thought she could run.

I actually don't know if the next part of this story is 100 percent true and I cannot fact check it. In my heart of hearts, it is how I remember it. It is certainly my truth. It was time for the annual Presidential Fitness Awards. For those old enough to remember this, can we just say thank you for all of the therapy this triggering competition had each year? It was as if middle school wasn't traumatic enough. To this day, I cannot do a pull-up or climb a rope without remembering the embarrassment of having too much body fat and not enough upper body strength to make the cut.

I digress. In this particular year, we had to run a mile on the outdoor track. I don't recall running a full mile in years prior or even what grade I was in when this happened. Only that I was deathly afraid of not being able to finish. A mile seemed like a very long distance to run, especially as a non-runner. When it came time to run, I lined up with a pit in my stomach. It is odd how I can still remember that feeling while other memories of the day are blurry at best. The stopwatch started. My feet began moving. I'm not exactly sure what happened next, other than I didn't stop running. In that moment, running seemed easy. Somehow, I ended that run with the best time for girls in my individual gym class. It was a humbling moment that I chalked up to sheer luck. When some friends joined track, I immediately passed. Track was for real runners, something I just wasn't built to do. This competition would come up again several years later and I'd find myself in the back of the pack – a place that I'd spend many years believing I belonged. After all, fat girls don't run. It'd be years before I'd ever consider running a race again.

One night, over 25-years later, I'd drink a few too many mojitos. Isn't that how most great stories start? I was with some of my more athletic friends, and while not athletic, I'm certainly competitive. I soon found myself proclaiming that I was training for a half-marathon. Truth be told, I was not. I didn't even own a pair of running shoes. My husband gave me that look. If you know, you know. The one of what the hell are you talking about? He swears he didn't. Perhaps it was the sun in his eyes. But what I saw was him mocking me – suggesting that I could never run a half-marathon. It was on. Short of me dying (or losing a toenail), I knew I'd run a race. I just didn't know how. I could have easily walked away. Nobody but me really cared that I had claimed to be a runner. Here's the thing. If I can find a way to make my life complicated. I do. Better yet if I can be miserable doing it. I think it is somehow programmed in my genes. Besides, I figured that if George Mallory could climb Mount Everest because "it is there" then I could run a half-marathon for equally as valid reasons and hopefully not die in my attempts.

The next day I started training under two conditions. I'd cross the finish line and retire the day I lost a toenail. A few months later I crossed the finish line at my first half-marathon. In-between the day I falsely proclaimed I was running a half-marathon and in fact waddled my way over the finish line, I dealt with many demons in my closet. Imposter syndrome took front and center that first time I walked into a specialty running store. I challenged whether my body was even capable of running that far. I seriously questioned if I might die come Mile 12. I feared other runners were judging myself, even though they were all too busy focusing on their own run to even notice I was there. I shit my pants. No seriously. I did. Literally. I laughed. I cried. But, most importantly, I finished the race for me.

A decade later, I'd write a book about the identity crisis that comes with being a back-of-the-pack fat runner. Much of the book focused in fact on my struggles of even calling myself a runner, despite having a wall of medals. I somehow managed to be interviewed in *Runner's World* about my insecurities. I talked about my running insecurities on *Another Mother Runner's* podcast and even contribute to their running blog. I'd complete over a dozen half-marathons, a series of 10k, 5ks obstacle runs and clock thousands of miles of training. Yet, I still struggled to call myself a runner.

Real runners win races. They make sacrifices to do something they love. They talk about a runner's high and count macros and skip evening cocktails for early morning runs. Running is a part of who they are—it is a piece of their soul. I sometimes hear my runner friends talk about how crazy they'd be without running, this somehow defines them. I envy their commitment and passion.

I think of my Instagram idols. Emma Coburn willingly voiced her disappointment after failing to medal in Tokyo. Kara Goucher's emotional roller coaster of navigating professional running and motherhood with grace and integrity, only to discover that her single greatest passion in life might be taken away due to illness.

My Instagram heroes don't stop with runners. I think of downhill skiing legend Lindsey Vonn racing down a mountain with her body patched together in a series of braces and grit. Or Nordic skier Jessie Diggin for her genuine passion for skiing to the point of sheer and utter exhaustion. These gals inspire me to seek out and discover my true passion. These are women to look up to.

Then there's me. The gal whose commitment to running ends with a broken toenail. I am just as likely to read a 300-page novel at the crack of dawn, or hike 5-miles to catch a sunrise and sip a latte as I am to lace up some shoes and go for a morning run. I've been known to count macros in mini donuts, consume deep friend cheese curds for calcium, and count hauling firewood and planting my garden as cross-training, stretching and conditioning all at once. I'm content to sip cocktails with friends, even if it means sacrificing a much-needed training run. Come Saturday, I don't hit snooze on my alarm. I don't even bother to set it. Sometimes that means bounding out of bed and running. Other times, it means rolling over and giving my body much needed rest.

For years, I battled with this notion of enough. Am I, in fact, enough?

Somewhere along the way, I was conditioned to believe that we all have a passion in life and we just need to find it. That there is some great adventure just beyond our reach that'll fulfill our every need. Cliches like it isn't work if you love it, follow your passion, discover your why and never give less than 100 percent. YOLO, right? No regrets?

I now call bullshit. For decades, I drank the Kool-Aid. I believed that somehow if you couldn't do it well, then you shouldn't do it at all. That somehow, less than perfect is half-ass and a waste of time. That I needed to be the best, because somehow anything less would be a disappointment to my parents. This, despite them loving me for who I am. The end result is when things have gotten tough, I've walked away. I somehow convinced myself that it is better to cut and run than lose. This served me well in some instances. It cost me in others. For whatever reason, when it came to running, I found that I kept showing up no matter how mediocre of a runner I was because I'd rather show up and finish last than never show up at all. Better yet, most days I feel good – heck – great about it. I've determined at least for me, that's what success looks like for me when it comes to running.

On a side note, if you're a good runner who finishes first and rolls your eyes right now because I'm not as committed to the sport as you – you're welcome. It is because of sloths like me that you can finish in the front of the pack. I'm also 99.9% convinced that those of us in the back of the pack have a heck of a lot more fun come race day than you. But, that's just me.

In all seriousness, though, what does this have to do with loss? I'll tell you what. In order for me to keep showing up at those starting lines, at some point, I had to acknowledge that I was in fact a runner.

That I in fact belonged. In order to do that, it meant letting go of my old identity of being too fat to be a runner. Of being this non-athlete who wasn't strong enough to run a half-marathon or frankly any race.

I still remember the day I started to believe I was a runner. It was 2019. My father had recently undergone an amputation that had serious complications. I had just switched jobs and was weeks away from graduating with my MBA in Rural Healthcare. The trifecta of stressors along with my kiddo entering kindergarten had me seeing a number on a scale I hadn't seen since my pregnancy days. I dealt with it like many folks in denial do – I scrolled mindlessly on Facebook. I won't get into the details but long story short, this scrolling ultimately led me to winning a guaranteed entry in the Garry Bjorklund Half-Marathon. The lottery-based half-marathon in Duluth isn't particularly difficult to get into but you do have to plan ahead and it is by far the largest race in my neck of the woods both in participants and spectators.

It also had a sweeper bus. As in, if you cannot finish within a certain time, a bus sweeps you off the course. I'm not sure if that's exactly how it plays out, but I do know you sign a waiver saying you're capable of finishing the race within a certain timeframe. I signed that waiver by justifying in my head that theoretically anything is possible. I then spent the next few months fearing that a large bus would force me to forfeit the race, at which point race officials would come face-to-face with a crazy Scandinavian who doesn't run 10-11 miles only to not receive her finishers medal and be escorted off a course for being too slow.

This bus, both physically and metaphorically, would force me to decide if I was ready to lose my old identity of fat girls don't run and acknowledge that perhaps my wall of finish line medals and worn out running shoes meant that maybe, just maybe, I was a runner. That, I should perhaps shed the limitations I'd set with those limiting beliefs and instead just acknowledge that yes, I'm a plus-size runner—with the focusing being runner.

Guess what? Come race day I ran the race in spite of the bus. I quit questioning whether I was a runner, and instead just ran for the love of running. On the course that day, a million thoughts raced through my head. I thought of my mom and how proud she'd be of me for not quitting. I ran for my dad who could no longer run. I ran for my son to show him that it isn't always about winning but instead showing up and trying. I ran for my friends who said my journey inspired them and convinced them to try something outside of their comfort zone. I ran for every fat girl who sits on the sidelines and thinks they aren't built to run. But most importantly, I ran for me because that's what real runners do. They run. I ended up setting a personal record that day. It wasn't enough to beat the cut-off time. But that damn bus that kept me awake for so many nights? It never even showed up. It turned out, I was a runner the day I started running.

Typing this, it sounds ridiculous. If we're being really honest with ourselves, though, how many of us have struggled with an identity crisis? Maybe it isn't running but something else. A few years after I crossed that finish line *Atomic Habits* would fall into my grubby hands. This book would literally change my life on so many levels. It took reading James Clear's words of wisdom to finally understand the impact identity has on the outcomes in my life. More importantly, once one identifies themselves a certain way, their actions follow.

The truth is, once I quit saying I was too fat to be a runner, I found myself running more. Now, it isn't unusual for me to just go outside and do a quick run, even if I'm not training for a race. I've applied this to a lot of other aspects of my life. Slowly but surely, I have reprogrammed myself to believe that I am in fact a runner. Sure, I occasionally revert back to my old beliefs and hear myself saying that I waddle or walk or woggle. I try to give myself grace in those moments and remind myself that as long as I'm lacing up and heading out, I'm a runner. It seems silly, but when you apply this to other aspects of your life – when you truly understand that you are a product of your beliefs, you suddenly start to realize how damaging the negative self-talk – how limiting the I'm not is – how out of alignment it is to deny yourself your truth. I wish James Clear had come into my life about 30-years ago. The power of habits is not new but the context in which he helps me understand how to align my habits to create the life I crave changed my perspective on just about every aspect of my life.

Chapter 13
Motherhood

About 4-months after the adoption failed, I started training for a half-marathon. It was just after the holidays in which in typical fashion I had overindulged in food and put exercise aside.

By this point in life, I had been running for a few years. A funny thing happened this time, though. My boobs hurt. As in, really hurt. At first, I thought that I'd jumped into training too hard. But as the days progressed and the spasms in my boobs grew more frequent, I knew something was up. I was broken.

It wasn't just my boobs. I was exhausted. I was exhausted when I ran and when I didn't run. I was tired all day long and had no desire to get up in the morning. Granted, it was January in northern Wisconsin. It's hard to be motivated about anything during this dark, sub-zero stretch of hell known as winter. But this was different.

After several weeks of enduring this excruciating pain, I decided to take a break from running for a few days. I thought maybe if I reset myself and started over it'd get better. Only it didn't. It kept getting worse. I didn't know what to do anymore. I shared my discomfort with my husband. He looked at me perplexed and then asked a very simple but loaded question, "You aren't pregnant, are you?"

Time stopped. He knew I was not pregnant. I would know if I was pregnant. After all, I'd gone through years of trying to get pregnant. I'd undergone countless fertility tests, prayed to higher powers and visited multiple doctors. While my diagnosis wasn't dire, I clearly didn't get pregnant. We had just gone through a year of paperwork and tests to get approved to adopt in the state of Wisconsin, only to have it fail. This was in fact an extremely loaded question. Of course, I wasn't pregnant. Or was I?

My mind began racing. I had a stash of pregnancy test strips under the sink. It'd be quite simple to do a quick test and put this rumor to rest. But a big part of me didn't want to get my hopes up. I started to do the math in my head. Yes, my period was late. If I were a gambler, I'd be broke if I bet on the dates my period would hit. Sometimes it'd be weeks, other times months. Plus, with the stress of the holidays, it'd make sense I was late, right?

After several rounds of inner conversation that was slowly making me crazy, I decide to take a test. I've got nothing to lose. At least then I can rule out this particular crazy notion. I take the test. After a few minutes I glance at the test strip. I see a couple of lines and dismiss the notion. I knew I wasn't pregnant.

A little while later, while nursing my sore boobs, my heart starts racing. I return to the bathroom and dig the test strip out of the garbage. Two lines. Is it possible that meant I was pregnant? I dig under the sink for directions. They're missing. I start to panic. How can I not remember if two or three lines mean I'm pregnant?!?!?!

Before you consider me a very dumb blond, remember the circumstances. Factor in that I purchased these test strips three years ago in bulk on Amazon. They didn't come in a pretty box. These strips didn't have smiley faces or pink lines. They were test strips with multiple faint lines.

I immediately turned to Google looking for answers. After finding directions online, my life changed in an instant.

"Honey..."

"Yeah?"

"I think I might be pregnant."

Silence. I can hear my husband carefully formulating a sentence in his brain before speaking, knowing the next words he speaks count.

"What do you mean you think you might be pregnant?"

"Well, this test says I'm pregnant, I think."

"You think? Isn't it a yes or a no?"

"Well sort of. But I'm guessing this test is expired."

Chaos ensued. My husband ran to our local grocery store, the only spot in town with pregnancy tests at the time, and asks the clerk for a pregnancy test. In the meantime, I Google what can cause a false positive. It'd appear that a rare form of cancer and a lot of urban myths are the only options. The sparkling optimist in me becomes convinced that I have cancer.

My husband returns home. "Well, either everyone in town tomorrow will know you're pregnant, or a rumor will be floating around that I'm having an affair." The joys of small-town living.

I guzzled water. Lots and lots of water. Three tests later, I'm starting to come to terms with the idea that I may, in fact, be pregnant. My husband is beaming and totally convinced this is the only possibility. I'd like to believe this miracle is real, but the pessimist in me refuses. I need scientific proof. Luckily, I have an awesome doctor and work at a rural hospital that can do same-day appointments.

Less than 24 hours later, I find myself lying on an ultrasound table at work, hearing a rapid pitter-patter, for the first time. It turns out that there was a logical explanation besides cancer for the nagging pain in my chest. His name is Jacob William Probst. At the time, I was six weeks pregnant.

In an instant, life changes but everything stays the same. I look down at my paunch and realize there's an alien-looking creature growing inside of me. That every decision I make in the coming months impacts the creation of another human being.

I'm humbled and overwhelmed and scared. Let's face it. This didn't happen overnight. I had come to terms with the idea of never having a baby. I'm old in childbearing age. Did you know that if you are 35 and pregnant, that's considered a geriatric pregnancy?

I've never quite understood the marketing of that. Adult pregnancy, mature pregnancy, but geriatric? It is very similar to wedding dresses being two sizes SMALLER than your normal size. Because seriously, what girl doesn't want to feel old when she's pregnant or fat on her wedding day?

I face the facts. I'm a plus-size, geriatric pregnant gal who was not planning to get pregnant this year. I had abandoned the prenatal vitamins and hadn't exactly been alcohol free over the holidays. Plus, the sugar cookies. So many sugar cookies. I just booked a trip to Washington D.C. for March and now this?

I confide with a few co-workers. Those closest know what a toll the adoption took on me. They get it. As I'm telling them the news, it finally hits me. I am actually pregnant. This is exactly what I wanted. Wasn't it?

My pregnancy would be plagued with complications. An achy back and an uncontrollable bladder eventually led to a more serious diagnosis of pre-eclampsia. In rural Wisconsin, this diagnosis played out in a 75-minute ambulance ride with three strange men, no shoes, and a heightened hormonal state. Our destination – the nearest trauma center equipped with a NICU.

It resulted in one of the most undramatic, dramatic results in my life. I never went into labor. I stabilized. After two nights of monitoring and Steve eating delicious looking take-out in front of me I was allowed to return home with strict orders of bedrest. I'd spend the next two weeks anxiously awaiting Jake's arrival while also questioning if I was capable of becoming a mother.

Motherhood is a pivotal moment that plays out over the course of years. I'll be frank, when Jake made his overly dramatic entrance into the world during an emergency c-section that involved him not only wrapping his umbilical cord around his neck but also somehow knotting it, I didn't feel an immediate sense of joy. I was in utter shock.

Moments later he was placed on me to nurse. Splayed out on the table, I felt like a unique combo of a milking cow and Humpty Dumpty being stitched back together. I just wanted a full fat vanilla latte with extra whip cream.

Staring down at the vulnerable mini me, I knew I was witness to a miracle. I was torn between the sheer excitement of this incredible creature I had just brought into the world and scared shitless of everything I could do wrong. In that moment, I needed my mom. Not my best friend or my sister or even the man who helped make Jake.

I knew giving birth would trigger the loss of my mother. I just didn't know how lost I'd feel those first few weeks. Hormones and sleepless nights didn't help. Unlike some incredible women I know, motherhood did not come naturally to me. It was awkward, uncomfortable and extremely complicated. I quickly learned that motherhood is messy.

Messy and memorable. Somewhere in those sleepless nights, something clicked. I suddenly understood what it meant to love someone so selflessly that you'd sacrifice everything for them.

There's something to be said about a love that fierce. I grew up in a house full of grace. I now understand why. My mother's love was built around the notion that I was exactly who I needed to be – not perfect – but enough. My mother never tried to change me and constantly gave me the freedom to make mistakes. To learn, grow and evolve into a young woman.

When Jake was born, I felt an unbelievable pressure to not mess it up. To make sure I raise him to be an incredible man. I now understand that I am not raising a child, but rather guiding a human being through life. Jake is his own person and to think I can change that is hilarious. I can guide and steer and pray and love, but at the end of the day Jake will become who he is destined to be. That's humbling and scary and awesome, all wrapped into one. To love someone enough to let them become who they are meant to be – that's the greatest gift I can give as a mother. One I learned from the best.

Motherhood is the ultimate test of vulnerability and loss. Lots of it. The thing with motherhood is loving someone unconditionally comes at a cost. It's an emotional rollercoaster of highs and lows. The more vulnerable and deep your love, the larger the tidal waves. I never understood mamas who cried on the first day of school or became insomniacs in a quest to make sure their child was safe until I became one. Every day I find myself loosening my grip on my son a bit more as he becomes an independent little man. To love him, is to let him go over and over again.

I went into parenthood believing I'd be the best mother ever. As a perfectionist, I wanted to be a perfect mom, because I wanted Jake to have the best. What mother doesn't? Here's the thing, by day one, I had failed on many fronts.

This seems obvious now but I didn't know it then. I am raising a human. Humans are messy, complicated and contradictory. They make mistakes. They are frustrating and difficult and stubborn and that's what makes them beautiful. Now, I just do my best every day to lead by example, love him, and set him free to be his own person. It is the single hardest thing I've ever done.

Is it perfect? Absolutely not. His teacher recently told us, Jake's an incredible leader. He just sometimes leads in the wrong direction. I'll admit, I was a bit embarrassed but bursting with pride and love. Raising Jake has taught me, I'll never be ready to parent a person but I was born to be a mom.

Chapter 14
Corona What?

It was one of those moments that seemed mundane at best. I found myself asking a co-worker, "Corona what?" It's late February, 2020 and there's a buzz about a virus that seems to be gaining momentum in the United States and at my workplace. My latest job is in healthcare – a Community Health Center that covers about 20,000 square miles of rural northern Wisconsin.

Just to be clear, I'm not a provider. I write grants and do marketing, so I often find myself asking super basic questions so I can attempt to simplify information for the communities we serve. At the time, information on this new virus was scarce, but folks on the operations team were speculating about the potential impact. I on the other hand was still trying to remember what the virus was called and how to spell it.

At times, the speculation seemed like the plot to a box office movie. The virus itself, which looked like a cross between an aquatic animal and a villain in a Disney movie, seemed surreal. I chalked it up to something that'd pass in a few months but that I should be vaguely aware of and track. I scribbled a note down to add the term to my google alerts and to be on the look-out for any updates from the Wisconsin Department of Health Services, in case it made its way to the Midwest.

We all know what happened next. Shit became real, really quick. A few days later the meetings started. Then contingency planning. Google alerts began blowing up my email with endless updates. Spring break was just a week away and my husband decided to pull the plug on our vacation. I was livid. I knew the virus was serious but we had waited over a year for this vacation. I was sun deprived and needed a work break. I consulted with some co-workers. It quickly became clear that a cross-country flight was a bad idea. I reluctantly albeit a bit passive aggressively agreed to the decision. A day later, the World Health Organization deemed COVID-19 a global pandemic. I'd find myself never again asking how to say or spell coronavirus again.

In an instant, everything changed but nothing changed. Work became incredibly busy. School kept going but I wasn't sure from day-to-day if the building would be open or if I'd have to home school my son. By home school, that meant shipping Jake off to day-care in hopes he'd be safe. We still needed toilet paper and dinner on the table, but we weren't sure if it'd be available when we went to the store. Living in rural Wisconsin, curbside shopping, Uber Eats and at-home delivery was not a thing. We navigated the best we could.

I watched friends lose their job, lose a parent and find themselves sick or laid up in bed for weeks with long-term COVID-19. COVID-19 had no rhyme or reason. Careless individuals seemed to avoid the virus, while others who limited human contact and went to great lengths to keep their family safe were hit hard.

At first, people were kind. We were *stronger together* and neighbors helping neighbors. We cheered for healthcare workers who worked overtime managing a disease they didn't understand and applauded frontline workers for making minimum wage to make sure there were groceries in everyone's fridge. Despite watching utter destruction, I watched countless individuals find the good in this global pandemic – to somehow suggest that perhaps this was the reset the world needed. A lot of time and energy was spent finding meaning in the madness. People baked bread, grew gardens and talked about returning to simpler times. We basked in rediscovering family dinners, puzzles and coloring. The pandemic shall pass – and when it does, we'll be better because of it. If only it were that easy.

As the months waned on, a subtle shift became apparent and a new debate took center stage. The debate over wearing a mask became a political platform about our freedoms and government's ability or inability to intervene in a public health emergency. If you home schooled your child, you were overreacting and risking the mental well-being of your child. If you sent your kid to school, you were endangering their life. It reached a point where everywhere you turned; COVID-19 was the topic of conversation. I found myself walking on eggshells wondering who I'd offend or disappoint next. Somehow this global pandemic went from being something we were going through together and instead became an *us versus them*, only I still have no clue who *they* are.

It was about this time that Jake turned 7. It was August, 2020. COVID-19 cases were relatively low in Bayfield County, Wisconsin. It was the height of summer and we thought an outdoor party was a possibility. We worked with our local pizza shop to make individual pizzas, purchased individually wrapped desserts and chose a public beach where there was plenty of space for social distancing. We invited Jake's closest friends and respected the parents who politely declined due to COVID-19 concerns. Then, the night before, my husband learned he was exposed to someone who was exposed to someone with COVID-19. We received the automated text from the local public health department. Irrational as it might sound, I was devastated and pissed off beyond belief.

Honestly, I wanted to ignore that text and proceed with the party as planned. I was tired of these disruptions and found myself justifying actions that I might very easily judge others for doing. Self-justification, rationalizing the irrational, whatever you want to call it. Ultimately, we knew we couldn't go through with the party knowing that we might have been exposed. We cancelled. It was yet another loss in COVID-19. In retrospect, it was not a major loss, but it was one more to add to a growing list of deficits. I started to wonder at what point, this global pandemic would leave an irreversible impact on my son's mental health. My mind started spiraling down the road of what ifs. My phone dinged.

It was my neighbor. She knows Steve had potentially been exposed and everyone's been notified. Ever the party planner, she and one of Jake's daycare teachers and family friends had come up with a plan b. In the time my mind spiraled out of control, convinced the pandemic would ultimately destroy my family, the duo planned a drive-by party at the local baseball field for Jake. Sure, my neighbor loves any reason to plan a party and she's great at rallying the troops. Yes, I live in a small-town where it isn't unusual for folks to come together when things get tough. But, this? It seemed impossible. There are no words I can possibly text to express my gratitude.

"The kids deserve a party," she explained. In her world, it was that simple. Where there is a will, there is a way. A simple work around. A way to rally around each other safely and make sure that Jake's 7th birthday party is one we will never forget.

The next day, Jake sits on the pitcher's mound in a bright blue chair adorned with helium balloons. A large banner filled with photos and well wishes hangs off the fence. Kids run by him and give him presents and eat individually wrapped ice cream drumsticks. They loudly sing Happy Birthday and just before piling in their cars and leaving, they launch dozens of water-filled balloons his way. He doesn't even see it coming. As quickly as it starts, it comes to a close. To this day, this party that almost wasn't, is by far one of his favorites. My heart is filled with gratitude.

A few months later, COVID-19 will rear its ugly head again. This time, in an attempt to keep my father safe, it'll force him into isolation at his independent living facility. A vaccine is on the way. If we can just make it through the holidays, he'll be first on the list. For nearly a year he's been lucky. Confirmed cases have been non-existent in the 40+ apartment complex where he resides. Staff have worked tirelessly to keep residents socially distanced, visitors at a minimum and sick staff at home. This couldn't last forever. It was bound to happen. Cases were confirmed. Residents are put in lockdown. It is isolation, not COVID-19, that dims the light in my father's soul.

A stubborn infection on my father's remaining leg refuses to heal, hinting at another amputation on the horizon. My father is clear that if it comes to that, he does not believe he'll survive. A routine transfer from wheelchair to recliner results in a brief cracking sound – something so mundane it is not even worth mentioning to his nurse.

We later learned it was a hairline fracture in his shoulder. The next day, my father would mention feeling off. Staff who know him well know he doesn't complain. They immediately ship him off to the local hospital.

It marks the beginning of the end. Once admitted to a local community hospital he'd be isolated from everyone he knows and loves for nearly 2-weeks. COVID-19 protocol prohibits us from being present during important diagnosis, treatment plans and information sharing. It is more than just the hairline fracture physicians discover, but we wouldn't learn that until much later. When my father needed his family most, there was no magical neighbor who could offer us a solution.

We did the best we could. Our family advocated from a distance. Fought when needed. Asked tough questions. The frontline healthcare workers we once applauded, we now understood were burned out and frustrated. My dad needed to be transferred. They needed the bed. The Thursday before Christmas they transferred him on to a skilled nursing facility with incomplete paperwork. A series of unfortunate events would seal my father's fate. Within a few days in the facility, he'd be carted off in an ambulance to the local Emergency Department in Duluth. From there he'd be transferred to an intensive care unit.

A different hospital meant different protocols. For the first time in weeks, we're allowed at my dad's bedside. He is a changed man. All hope is gone. He is done fighting. Whether it was fate, circumstance, time or a combination of all three, the outcome is the same. I think for years my father had held on to intrinsic hope. A quality of life centered around connections with his family and neighbors. The ability to live independently even though he could no longer drive or walk. COVID-19 stripped that away.

We all know how this story ends. Dad dies a few days later alone. But, by the grace of God, an Angel, my mother or just sheer luck, we're able to say goodbye in person. I get to hold his hand and give him one final hug. I get to tell him I love him and that it is alright that he is ready to go. That I am not angry, just sad that I'll have to live without him. I get to share one last popsicle with him and my sister. I get to watch him make the decision to go on his terms and on his timeline. Later, in hospice, I'll have a moment alone with him. He can no longer argue about the price of a ribeye or gas. Instead, enough morphine is pumped into his body that he's peaceful. Halfway to whatever comes after. Again, COVID-19 has collectively taken so much away but has given me a special appreciation and gratitude for this moment. I leave nothing left unsaid.

When the vaccine becomes available, I watch as some people clamor to get it while others curse the government convinced it'll kill them. It's such a polarizing response to a global event that's found a way to divide our country. Or at least convince us we're divided. Yet, when I turn off the news or ignore the trolls and spammers and talk to my friends and neighbors, I find we're all very similar.

We're tired of COVID-19. We all experienced loss. We were afraid. We navigated the unknown to the best of our ability. We did the best we could with the information we had available at the time. We made calculated choices that were not black and white because life is not black and white. Sometimes we took risks that were nec-essary, other times we doubled down on what we believed was safe in hopes of keeping this global nuisance from hitting those we love. In both cases, there were wins and losses. We got lucky or were dealt harsh consequences that had no rhyme or reason.

It will be decades before we fully understand the impact

COVID-19 has had on our lives. What I do know is that the collective grief that so many of us experienced during the height of COVID-19 wreaked havoc on our lives that'll never be forgotten.

Chapter 15
Crow's Feet

After my dad died, I found myself obsessed with mortality. A number of factors were at play. The year marked a pivotal moment for so many reasons beyond becoming an orphan. I also turned 44 – a seemingly insignificant number unless you factor in the facts of my life.

I celebrated an anniversary with my husband that surpasses the number of years I had with mom. It was the first time in my life where I had chosen to be with someone longer than I was with my mom. It was inevitable but strange to recognize that the man I wake up next to each day likely knows me better than the woman who birthed me. That I had spent more time loving him than my mom had to love me. I distinctly remember the day my mom died – she was 47. That seemed ancient to my 18-year-old self. My how times change.

This tender age also triggers the age my mom was when I started to notice she had problems. I was old enough to remember my mom turning 44. It was about this time the puzzle pieces began popping up around me as she battled her demons with weight, alcohol and mental illness. I wasn't old enough to understand what was happening. It'd take years for me to piece it altogether. Now I understand and suddenly I fear repeating history.

It keeps me awake some nights – wondering if I will somehow become her. It certainly guides me to pass on alcohol if I'm having a bad day and to double down on mindfulness practices and self-care. As for the weight loss journey, ask me if there's ever been a time in my adult life where I wasn't struggling with my weight. I do my best not to participate in the self-loathing that goes with the intensely dangerous diet culture we are all subjected to too. I am also human and desire to weigh less. For now, my unhealthy relationship with my body is not deadly but at times depressing. That, in of itself, is an entirely different book.

The day I turn 44 I'm in California enjoying spring break with my family. We stayed in San Francisco and I thoroughly soaked in the California sun while sipping on a margarita and feasting on fresh seafood at Fisherman's Wharf. We explored Chinatown and played arcade games. It was the perfect birthday.

It was also the first birthday that I felt legitimately old. As in, aging. To some extent, even finite. It doesn't help that when I look over at my little boy, I see a mini-man growing up much too fast. I realize that my guaranteed parenting days are almost half-way done and that before I know it, my 8-year-old will be 18 and potentially moving out.

Don't roll your eyes at me and tell me I'm young. I know I'm only 44 and it is all about perspective but this reality combined with a series of events have reminded me that I am no longer a spring chicken.

First, there's the pandemic pounds that have piled up in my

mid-section thanks to perimenopausal (and over-indulging). Then, age, or spending endless days in virtual google meetings, resulted in so much squinting that I finally broke down and saw an optometrist. Cheaters were the solution, for now. A series of ads resulted in me noticing the deep divots (likely from squinting) lining my forehead and a flock of crow's feet on my eyes. A custom skincare promises to ease the problem, or at least inform my ego I'm trying to slow the decline. These items would be bad enough, but manageable. It gets worse.

Shooting hoops with my kid makes my plantar fasciitis flare up and running has become increasingly difficult. My last 5k was my worst time ever. I could blame the 25 mph winds and sleet, but if I'm being honest, I'm slow. Racing on an indoor track this past winter, my kid beat me. A part of me told myself and him that I let him. That isn't entirely true. I've also found myself flinching when we practice baseball, fearful that my reflex time won't be responsive enough and I'll find myself with a broken jaw or bruised shins. Again, one could reason all of this away. To say that as you age, of course you get slower as a runner. That said, as someone who is the back of the packer to begin with, there is certainly room for me to up my fitness game and improve my time. If only. Two words that are a bit destructive but necessary at this point in my life.

I've noticed I'm not as quick to spring up after lounging on the couch. Odd cracking sounds usually follow. Muscles are tender. Hair is thinning. My memory isn't quite as crisp.

My husband also informed me, while vacationing in California, that I snore. He even took video to prove his case after I spent months denying this accusation. I'm sure this is a result of any number of the above items, including but not limited to the pandemic pounds.

At Easter, I feast on my favorite candy. Mini Cadbury eggs one can devour like crack. You know the ones I'm talking about, the pastel-colored chocolate eggs with the hard outer shell. The shell slipped under my 20+ year old crown. I attempted to dig it out – and pop – my entire tooth came flying out. A consult with a dentist along with a second opinion leaves me with a year-long treatment plan consisting of multiple surgeries and a $6,000 implant bill to pay.

I hope this is an isolated incident but visions of dentures dance through my head. I contemplate a soft food diet moving forward. This lasts until dinner time. I've consulted with my physician and invest in some vitamins and supplements. I sometimes wonder if these are just placebos to cater to one's ego, similar to my new facewash routine. Time will tell. Right now, this laundry list of ailments is manageable and even laughable most days. Some hard work and commitment can reverse some of the most dangerous ailments, the others, I'm adjusting too.

Bottom line. I'm aging. With aging comes perspective and an appreciation for my mortality. My finitude. There was a time in my life where I would have given anything to reduce the wrinkles, lose the weight and stay young forever. It is the same version of me that would gladly wish away my grief.

Here's the thing, memories and aging go together like love and grief. Wrinkles, stretch marks, creaky bones and fading eyesight mean I've been granted time on this planet to make memories. Don't get me wrong, I lived a charmed life growing up. I wouldn't trade my childhood for anything. I also wouldn't trade this aging body for anything.

The things that have aged me are what make life worth living. My son exhausts me every day. The endless questions, redirecting, and attempts to keep him safe and alive leave little in my gas tank come nightfall. The scar on my stomach surrounded by stretch marks

– entirely him. My inability to sleep through the night due to a broken bladder, him, and maybe some extra weight.

I think about the man I've now been with for nearly two decades. Like any relationship, we've had our ups and downs. The two balance each other out and remind me how blessed I am. How lucky I am to have someone to share this crazy, unpredictable life with, that I chose.

Then there's grief. The best friend you some days wish you never met.

I start to connect the dots. After dad died, I noticed some reoccurring themes. People who wanted to share in their loss with me – to talk about the death of their father or family member. They could relate because they too were reckoning with the hard reality that the longer you love someone and the more connected you are, the more it hurts to lose them. I naively thought when I said good-bye to dad, this would be easier than mom. That somehow, because we had more time, I'd find meaning in his absence sooner. That I could perhaps even skip grief altogether. That somehow manifesting away my feelings would result in me moving past this painful moment quietly and quickly. Ignorance is bliss. Instead, grief kicked me in the ass hard. It hurt. I let it. Perspective and perhaps a case of the fuck its, allowed me to feel my pain. This time, there was no performance for others. I was hurt. What daughter who loved her dad wouldn't be? Instead, I tried to be honest.

There were also people visibly uncomfortable with my vulnerability. At times, they appeared almost angry with my inability to move on. Some were bold in their statements, hinting that I should feel blessed to have had as much time with him as I did. Others, not understanding why this weighs so heavily, hinted that it shouldn't hurt as much since I knew it was coming. That somehow those extra days with him should have erased any of the grief that followed in his passing. I struggled with how to explain that I can grieve my loss while also being relieved he is no longer suffering – that I do not live in a world of ultimatums.

I get it. We live in a world where pain is uncomfortable. As is aging. Parenting. Marriage. Anything where one must reckon with the good and the bad. I had 43-years with dad. It was, as Charles Dickens would say, "the best of times and the worst of times."

That's what life is all about, though. As I try to find grace in my aging, I find myself wishing to slow that aging process down just a bit by being present. Not halting it, changing it, or rushing it. Instead, just being present in the moment. I've realized my body and time here is finite. Much is out of my control. What isn't, I should cherish because someday, perhaps soon, I'll wish for this body back.

Divinity professor and cancer warrior Kate Bowler so elegantly points out that so often life just doesn't add up. This coming from a woman who had it all, right, until she was diagnosed with Stage 4 cancer. In her book, *No Cure for being human (and other truths I need to hear),* Bowler said, "It takes great courage to live. Period. There are fears and disappointments and failures every day, and, in the end, the hero dies. It must be cinematic to watch us from above."

Despite witnessing the finitude of life around me, grappling with one's own mortality is harder. To acknowledge that someday, my time will be up. That there is frankly no rhyme or reason to when the Universe says today is your day. Sometimes, that understanding is bittersweet. It causes me to question if I'm doing enough to leave my mark in the world while at the same time acknowledging the world will go on without me.

Chapter 16
Reckoning

"Please don't take it out on us, but we didn't do our job," the Minnesota Department of Health investigator said.

Many words followed this sentence. Many questions were finally answered. It was April 2022, more than 15-months years after my father died. After a tumultuous ride of government bureaucracy, I finally fully understood the final 3-weeks of my father's life. I frantically scribble some notes about what the Department of Health nurse found when investigating the days leading up to my father's death.

The journey to these answers was anything but smooth. Fifteen months prior I had asked the simple question, why? Leading up to my father's death, there were countless times I thought he might not make it. After all, his health was complicated at best. Fifteen months following that simple question, investigation findings are provided to me. An investigator apologizes for her predecessor and the agency not doing their job. She asks me not to hold it against them. She informs me of other options – other ways I could pursue justice and peace via a process packed with more paperwork and headaches. I appreciate her kindness but immediately dismiss the notion. Litigation and citations were never my intent. I just wanted to understand, to be given the truth and to believe that in my father's final days he was treated with dignity. He deserved that – regardless of a pandemic.

As she provided additional options, I find I'm angry as hell. Not at her, or our broken healthcare system. I'm angry with myself. I'm disappointed that I didn't do more or advocate more or somehow make the providers listen to our family's pleas for help. Hindsight is like that – always showing you the cracks in the system and what you could have and should have done. The findings do not help.

For fifteen months, I played those final days out over and over again in my head. I know it is dangerous. That regret, without moving forward, is a miserable way to live life. The thing is, no matter what, if I play the whole story out, the conclusion is always the same. If not then, then when?

My dad was not invincible, despite defying the odds countless times. We shared more birthdays, Father's Days and conversations about the price of meat than I ever thought possible. I asked questions, was by his bedside that final day and got to say good-bye, despite it being a global pandemic. I do not take any of that for granted. I know many, many people who were not as fortunate.

This information explained my dad's final days and what led to his fateful decision. Equally as important, I understand that my father had complete agency over his decision. He fought battles much tougher than this and for whatever reason, this time he was ready. He wouldn't want me to be angry about the system or myself. Instead, he'd want me to know that this was his choice to make. He made it while he could – the ultimate final gift to his daughters – better him to make the choice than put us in the position of having to make it for him. It doesn't make grieving easier, but it helps me understand something that'll never completely make sense.

I've experienced a range of emotions ranging from numbness to forced acceptance, rage, relief and sadness these past 15-months. Many of these emotions replicate the stages of grief so commonly misunderstood. In this moment, I find myself in a place of peace. A place of remembering decades of moments we shared and not his final minutes. It is those memories that define him – us – our relationship. This is, after all, what he'd want me to focus on.

I remembered our fishing opener trips – including the time I was so engrossed in my book that a fish pulled my rod into the lake before I noticed I had caught it. Somehow dad managed to retrieve the rod with a very tired fish on it. I remembered my one successful day of catching Sunfish with dad and how delicious his pan-fried fish tasted. These fish are permanently mounted in my living room – a visual reminder of the special bond we shared.

I remembered our annual camping trips up north, our road trip out west, and the endless county and state fair trips growing up. I'm reminded of the look. You know – the one that only a dad can give that says a thousand words. I didn't get it often, but there was a time I flicked matches into his ice shanty to burn it down because I was obsessed with fire and then lied about it, not to mention the time I got removed from a little league softball game for being sassy. In both of those cases, the look was much harsher than the words that followed.

I remembered arguing over the cost of a good steak, grapes and a 12-pack of Diet Coke more than once. I remembered the endless conversations about weather where only Google could resolve the temperature differences between my dad's house in Minnesota and my house in northern Wisconsin. I remembered arguing just to argue and then arguing about why we were arguing, only to have my dad ask why I was so irritated. My dad loved a good debate about nothing and loved to rile up anyone who would entertain his random ramblings. That trait lives on in me.

I remembered the endless days of playing ball growing up. Or how dad would patiently watch me twirl the baton, doing his best not to comment on the fact that I was destroying the lawn with my endless pivots in a quest to land that double turn around. He always made time for this even after working a double shift at the local paper mill to ensure we had the money needed to support these endless hobbies.

I remembered helping him plant his garden and sharing that first ripe summer sweet pea. I remembered our trips to the Chicken Swap that resulted in unconventional pets and dad buying me a mule named Goldie and trying to pass her off as a pony because I was sad the pony I had wanted got purchased before we could buy him.

There was the advice. Dad lecturing me on how I didn't need another degree to feel smart or that changing jobs wouldn't make me happy. That a job is called that for a reason. I remembered my wedding day where after our father-daughter dance he simply said if Steve made me happy, then he was happy for me. Or, the time he casually asked if I knew how babies were made when he felt I was taking too long to make him a grandpa again. I was 34 at the time.

I remembered dad telling me he missed mom too when he knew I was sad. I remembered dad walking me down the aisle at my wedding and holding my son after he was born. I remembered him helping me pack for college, seeing me off to Oxford and inspecting my first home. In every critical moment, dad was always there on the sidelines rooting for my success. He's been the constant in my life – a larger than life figure that helped fill the void that mom left me when I turned 18. For over 40-years, every major milestone was marked by dad encouraging me to pursue my dreams. Now suddenly, he's gone. I'm left to navigate these moments alone.

As I sit and remember, it is easy to understand the tidal waves of grief that come and go. After losing dad, I lost my mojo. It was almost as if a candle dapper was placed on my soul. No matter how hard I tried to shine, I simply couldn't. I questioned how long I could live in this limbo land of grief and sadness while still trying to show up for those I loved. At times, my grief would morph into rage, reminding me of the intensity of the love I carried for all things lost, but mostly my dad.

As time passed, I gave myself much needed space to grieve. I did my best to feel the sadness that welled up inside, while also making room for love, life and laughter to seep into my soul. My child's resilience and endless attempts to be a clown reminded me that laughter, while not a cure for grief, goes a long way in treating it.

I let myself feel the relief that comes with knowing my dad is no longer suffering, even if it means I'm without him. That I'm blessed in that I'm capable of holding space for both grief and relief. The stages of grief come and go, often times without warning. At some point along this long and winding journey, I've made peace with the process. I understand there is no end to grief, just evolution and understanding mixed with perspective and emotional multi-tasking. I acknowledge my conflicting emotions are just a reflection of the complexities of living a bold and beautiful life.

In my freshman year of college, a writing professor assigned my class to write about the most pivotal moment of our life. I've always hated the question. The answer that day was easy – losing mom. I knew life would never be the same without her. That I was in fact forever changed because I lost her. More than 25-years later, her loss still stings. She was the most influential person in my life. Her loss leaves a void that'll never be filled. That said, I no longer believe that life is defined in a moment – even one as painful as losing the person you love most.

It took me decades and multiple rounds of therapy to forgive myself for not helping my mom with laundry that fateful day back in 1996. The impact of that shame and burden is impossible to quantify but inevitably a factor in what makes me, me. At 18, I could not possibly understand the complexities of my mother's illness and what ultimately led to her death. Now, I find myself reconciling with my father's final days and whether I did enough. If I advocated hard enough when he needed us most. At least for now, I believe even in his darkest hours, he knew what he wanted, and we supported that. Good or bad, these moments are a piece of what I'll carry with me for the rest of my life. Certainly, a part of who I am but only a piece. I realize that life is complicated. Answers don't provide closure. There is no other side of grief. Instead, grief is the price of admission to a life well lived.

I could write pages on the ups and downs of my parents, but the heart of the story is I was blessed to have two parents who supported and instilled in me a huge sense of ownership, accountability and determination to create the life I wanted for myself. There were no silver spoon hand-outs or ribbons for finishing last. There was always space and acceptance for me to do me. I find myself in a full circle moment. What ultimately makes life memorable and meaningful is a series of small, inconsequential moments that equate to the life we live every single day. The most pivotal moment of my life is not an event but a gift. A gift both parents gave me to me. To love me for who I am. To show me their flaws – to be human and vulnerable and share their greatest fears with me and believe I will love them back. Complicated and downright messy at times, but what an incredible gift to leave behind. What better way to honor it than to grieve with grace.

Grief books recommend you not make life altering decisions after a major loss. I opted not to listen and instead placed a permanent reminder honoring the legacy they left behind. I ink Sisu on my wrist in memory of my parents and a reminder of who I am. Sisu, which is not translatable in English but is often described as *stoic determination, tenacity of purpose, grit, bravery, resilience, and hardiness* AKA Badass Finlander. The truth is, my parents instilled this in me from the day I was born. I've always known in my heart that this is who I am, but it took losing them to be proud enough to own it. May you all find your inner Sisu.

Epilogue

When I started writing this book, I was unsure where to start and end my story. Much of my adult life has been framed around love and loss. When the two collide, how does one know where to start and stop their story?

The truth is, as long as I keep living and loving, loss will follow. Loss is what makes space for something new. Loss is what provides pivotal teaching moments that I didn't ask for and often times didn't want. Loss reminds me how real and strong pain is, but yet I somehow persevere. Loss is what puts love in perspective.

After my mom died, I remember being angry at the clock. Angry that time kept ticking away even though my world had ended. I didn't want to get through it, find meaning or experience closure. I just wanted the immediate pain to end.

Since then, the most common question I hear from friends who recently lost their parents is, *does it ever get easier?*

Pinterest, Hollywood, licensed professionals and many self-help gurus will tell you yes.

I disagree.

It gets different. There will be days, months or years where your loss seems manageable. You might even momentarily forget the void in your life. Then, you'll find yourself walking in Walmart and catch a glimpse of a middle-aged woman that your brain believes is your mother. Without thinking, you will slowly but methodically trail this woman hoping some miracle is unfolding. She turns. In an instant that last remaining hope that you didn't even know was there is ripped away from you. Once again, you are reminded in real time that by definition, loss means she is gone forever. Sure, I sometimes feel her presence. It is never enough.

At 44, I've discovered forever is a long time. That each individual loss is unique in its own right but consistently hurts. Equally as amazing is the human ability to hold pain and joy simultaneously. I wish my 18-year-old self knew I could grieve the loss of my mother and enjoy life. That it wasn't an either-or choice. That loss didn't mean wearing black, frowning and putting a hold on my life. Or believing that if you rush through the pain and just grieve hard enough, joy awaits you. Or worse yet, shaming yourself for daring to be happy again. We are incredible creatures designed to emotionally multi-task, yet we often find ourselves forced to make a choice. I now understand that I can choose both.

I promise, you will laugh again. When you do, embrace it. When the pain returns, embrace it as well. As I said in the beginning, in the wise words of Winnie the Pooh, *"how lucky I am to have something that makes saying goodbye so hard."*

On days that are too hard and dark for Pooh's words of wisdom to carry yourself, dare yourself. Dare to keep living. To keep moving. To be vulnerable. To believe and understand and embrace that the human experience is packed with losses both great and small. Most importantly, give yourself grace. Ask for help when you need it and look within yourself to find strength. You do not have to do this alone.

Ultimately, I hope these stories provide you with some perspective and peace. Your journey of loss is entirely yours. I just ask that you find it within yourself to feel the loss but not lose yourself in the loss.

As for now, what? You decide.

Breath. Laugh. Cry. Scream. Journal. Take a shot (if you're 21 or above). Go for a hike. Read a book. Kiss the boy. Play ball. Assemble a puzzle. Sleep. Grow sunflowers. Polish rocks. Shower. Eat mozzarella sticks. Dance. Get a tattoo. A haircut. A pedicure. Walk your dog. Bike ride. Backpack. Camp. Run a half-marathon. Kayak. Write a book.

I did all of that and more. Eventually I slowly found myself living again. Challenge yourself to find a way to keep living life for you, in spite of your loss.

In return, I promise you the loss does not get easier. You get stronger.

Acknowledgements

To the people in my life who encouraged me to plow ahead publishing this book thank you. The truth is, this was a story I needed to share with the world but was incredibly difficult to put on paper. This is definitely a labor of love that wouldn't have come to fruition without you.

A special thanks to Nikki Kallio for your honest critique and edits, Brandi Craig for capturing the spirit of this book in your beautiful cover design, and to Kate Deering for designing another book with me, even after enduring nearly a decade of my friendship. You ladies inspire me with your creativity and talent.

To Steve for willingly allowing me to share a small window into our relationship and our family's life, thank you for understanding why this is important to me. To Jake for keeping me humble and reminding me daily what truly matters in life. To my sisters, who were a huge part of this journey. I couldn't navigate these ups and downs without you.

Lastly, to the individuals who supported my first book and are reading these words right now, thank you. I have a long way to go as a writer but know that it means the world to me to know that somewhere out there, someone may benefit from the truths I share.